HOW TO START A PROFITABLE
BLOG BUSINESS
THAT MAKES YOU MONEY

CREATING & SETTING UP
YOUR BLOG WEBSITE

SASHA EVDAKOV

TABLE OF CONTENTS

CHAPTER 1:
INTRODUCTION

Internet blogs have soared over the last five years. Blogs are still one of the best foundational concepts to getting a business running online.

You can use a blog as a gateway to your customers or you can use it to run a full-fledged business by creating offers and selling products.

The blog can be your foundation to having a lifestyle that you want if you have the knowledge of how to get your business off the ground and do the necessary tasks.

Before deciding on writing a book about creating a blog business, I heard the stories and complaints that many books were lacking substance. Often times, the information was surface level and never dove into the core concepts that are necessary to make a blog business profitable.

After purchasing and reading a handful of books about blogging, ranging from how to set up a blog, or how to make extra income online, I discovered that much of the information given was similar.

In this book and series, I will not be discussing the technical details and the little nuances that you can find in most books, on the web, or on YouTube. I will share some basics that are geared toward someone who is just getting started, but interested in having a foundation to create a profitable and successful blog business.

My goal with this book is to provide you with specific information on how to "create a business from blogging."

You have to think of blogging as a business rather than a place where you put up some posts sequentially every week.

This is one of the main reasons why many people fail in starting a blog business or making money online is that they have the wrong mentality about what they are doing.

A blog business is a lot of work!

There are many components that go into it and if you don't have the right things in place or the right foundation you will be another blogger who makes less than $500 a month.

Five-hundred dollars may not sound like a bad amount of money, but it's not a comfortable living for an average person.

If you want to quit your job working for someone else, give yourself additional income, have more free time to spend with your kids, or have location flexibility so that you can travel the world, then having an online blog business could give you exactly that so long as you put the right sequences and processes in place.

I'm not saying it's going to be easy.

It will take a great deal of work, time, and energy along with some money to get started. Running a blog business is one of the most cost-effective and low barriers to entry business endeavors. However, because of the low barriers it is time-consuming and can be energetically draining.

If you are willing to do the work, put the time into it, give a lot of energy into it, and do the necessary things – there is no reason why you can't make a decent living online from a blog business and have the additional perks that come with it.

As you read this book, think of the psychological processes that you have to go through. Think about the planning, the mindsets, and the tasks that you may have to do that are uncomfortable.

I will mention a handful of things that you have to take action on throughout this book. Some of them will be more difficult than others.

Push through the things that you don't understand, read more about them, or watch additional videos online. It will help put all the pieces together for you.

Now, I won't be covering everything in this book from A to Z like getting started to running a multi-million-dollar blog.

Instead, this book is about understanding and setting up the right foundation for creating a blog business. This way you can start on the right foot and properly setup the initial business concepts in place to launch your blog business.

Concepts like marketing, a step-by-step guide, or tips on traffic generation are broad topics that they could be their own books altogether.

Note: I have a book on marketing your blog business releasing soon if it's not out already. Look for it on Amazon. It's called *"Marketing Your Blog Business: Increase Your Website Traffic, Build Your Email List, & Sell More Products."*

Remember that if you have the right foundation, the rest of the things become easier. Now, depending on your time and flexibility, going through this book and actually executing some of the steps may take you a week and for others, a few months.

Take things at your own pace. This is a long-term turtle race. A business, whether it is a brick and mortar or an online business takes time to develop. It is not a get rich quick scheme.

At times you may need to come back to some sections and reread them. The best approach to take is to read the book once all the way through and then let things soak in.

In a few days, pick up the book again and go through it a second time as you execute some of the steps.

Let's get it started!

How it all started for me

By now you may have read a handful of books regarding blogging and how to make money with a blog.

Everyone's blogging journey is different and every successful blogger or online business owner probably had a different path and sequence of steps that got them there.

We all have different specialties, expertise, and strengths. You need to utilize all these components when building your blog business.

Fortunately for me, I had an easier start with blogging than most people. You could say I fell into it at an early age.

I've never had a traditional job before as I've always worked for myself. Blogging was my first big break through. After starting my blog business, this is where things accelerated immensely.

Since I've never had a traditional job, I can never title any of my books "How I quit my day job and make money blogging full-time," but that is beside the point.

My blogging career started out through other passions. We all have multiple passions and hobbies that we enjoy. Eventually one thing may lead to another.

Here is an example of a linear path with three different areas of focus in one's life.

These sequences are infinite and can continue for a long time. Other sequences may merge and some may actually die off.

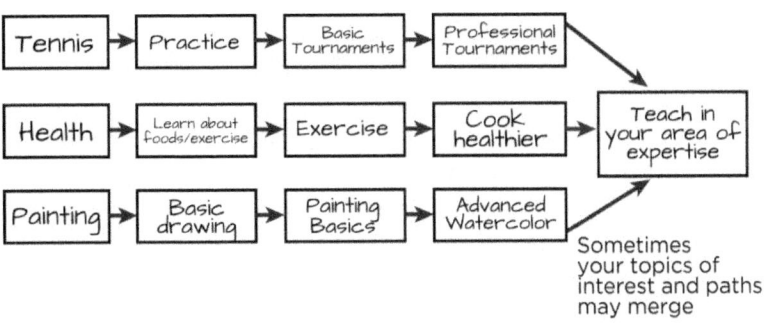

For me, I had a few hobbies when I was young. I enjoyed tennis, karate, technology, drawing, academics, and learning. You could say my biggest drive was to learn. It fascinated me.

I combined multiple areas of my life such as technology, drawing, and passion to learn to come up with a new hobby or business.

The reason for this is because by the time I was 13 years old, I started doing logos, graphic design, and websites. These earlier skills in my teenage years gave me a leg up on blogging when it started to go mainstream and by the time I hit my teenage years, I had my first blog.

However, just because I had success as a kid, don't let this fool you that the business part was easy.

There are three rules in life that I believe apply to everyone.

1. Everybody works
2. Nothing is free
3. Everybody starts at the bottom

My journey began in Russia. My earlier years in life were not easy – quite difficult in fact.

I was born in Siberia where we didn't have many of the standard things available to those in the USA. Money was tight.

In fact, we didn't even have plumbing. Many times we had to go wash ourselves at the neighbor's sauna or during summer months we used rags and buckets of water from the water well to clean ourselves off.

Due to this hardship, I became a motivated kid at a young age.

When my mom and I moved to Florida, I realized early on that I had to seize every opportunity. For this reason, starting a business flowed through my blood.

When I got my first computer at age 12, it was at that point that I decided to start my first business. After spending the first year playing games online I finally started being purposeful.

As a young kid, you don't get to be involved in big business because most people won't take you seriously. However, behind the Internet I was able to hide my age and it gave me a chance to break through the barriers to give me a taste of the business world.

I initially started my online income by designing logos for people on eBay and chat rooms. This led me to designing brochures and stationery.

After I became great at those things I was asked to create websites and then do some search engine marketing.

I was driven to learn and hungry for business.

As I progressed one of my friend's parents (Alan) asked me to design a diamond business website. He sold diamonds and wanted to leverage the power of the Internet to get his business online.

This is when I got involved in larger business dealings. I started to evolve and grow his website because I was receiving a percentage of the sales as payment for the work.

We created a diamond price calculator where we collected email addresses and phone numbers so that we could call them and get a chance to sell them diamonds. We even created a major article library.

By the time I was in my mid-teenage years, I decided to create my own diamond blog and library of information because of my own personal interest in diamonds, as we wanted to keep the diamond business separate from the diamond library.

Over the next few years, I contributed to writing and creating a few hundred blog posts on that website. At that time I called them articles, but really they were blog posts.

As time progressed, my web development business grew, I did some photography, I became extremely interested in the stock market, went to college, but I still kept up with my diamond blog. It was one of those side interests that I couldn't drop.

I placed advertisements on the website and it started to earn about $500 per month in my early college years and then eventually $1,500 per month. Keep in mind I was still getting commission for diamond sales from the other website I designed for Alan.

When the blog matured after a few years, I would say by the end of my college years, exposure was booming in my niche. My diamond library website was one of the largest diamond informational resources. I was listed in Wikipedia and many other large authority websites.

Due to this exposure, I had a few different offers to purchase the blog that came to my attention, but I never thought about it seriously until I got more into investing.

After a great deal of thinking and debating, the website was sold and that year, between the sale, ad revenue, and commissions I made over $100,000 from my blog. A very successful year I thought for something I maintained part-time.

Since then, I continue to blog because it brings me personal pleasure. I like the time freedom, I enjoy the freedom of speech, and sharing my ideas and concepts. I love teaching, creating products and not to mention, I am passionate about education.

To be transparent, I still do a great deal of investing and stock trading to grow my financial nest egg, but I can tell you that the blog businesses that I maintain generates a healthy income on its own.

Don't forget that this adventure is about creating a "blog business" rather than just a blog, and in this book I'm going to share with you the correct process, mindsets, and steps to set up the proper foundation for your blog business so that it pays you consistently.

Just like I mentioned the sequence of events earlier that continue to evolve the same thing happens in your life on a more complicated level.

Everything you've done previously in life builds to the next thing.

This, in the end, creates our life path. If you don't like your current path then you need to start building some skill sets and a great foundation to adjust your path.

My life path

Here's an example of my life path (a much larger view of various sequences) specifically focused on the business aspect of my life and how I have evolved from one thing to the next.

Maybe this will give you an idea to create your own path and draw it out.

Of course there are other little steps and sub steps that have happened in between and other hobbies that I enjoy, but in general this gives you an idea of how things moved in my life over the years and how it relates to building a blog business and creating wealth.

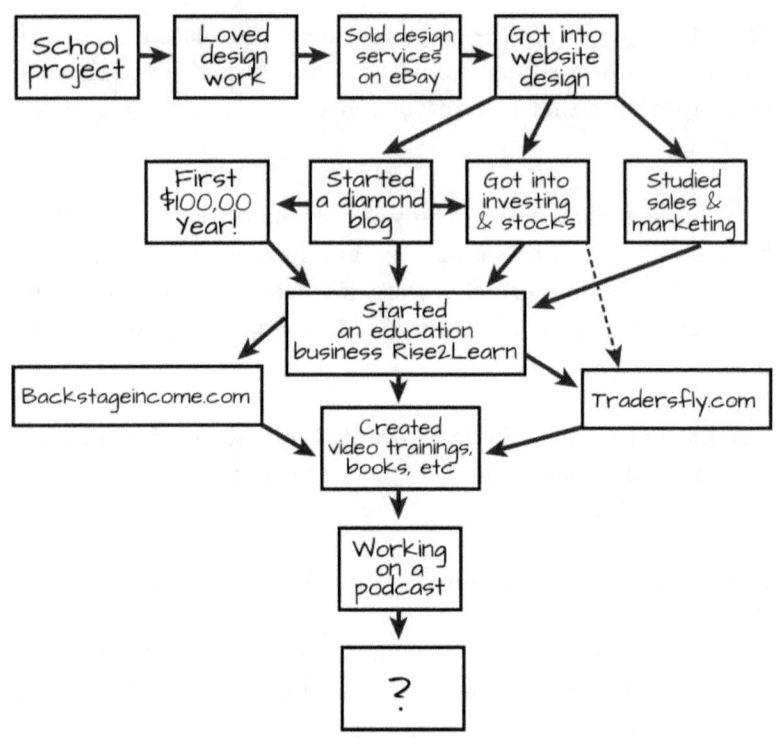

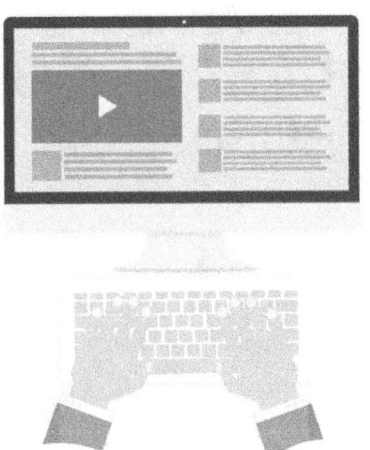

SECTION #1
KNOW THE BLOG
FOUNDATION

CHAPTER 2:
WHY CREATE A BLOG BUSINESS?

Before you start doing anything in life, it is important to know "why" you are doing it.

If you define the "why", you will know where to go or what to strive for. When you focus on the "why" you will know which things are critical to do and which things you can skip over. So my question to you is: why do you want to start a blog?

Over time I have found there are usually a few different reasons on why people are interested in blogging. The first and probably the main reason is that they think that blogging is easy money, in which case I will tell you that it is not!

There is no such thing as easy money.

On the flipside, blogging does allow additional benefits that you may enjoy.

Today, with the acceleration of billions of websites in the world the competition is intense.

We have websites for companies, products, opinions, communication, hate websites, video websites, and many other categories. In fact did you know there are more websites then there are people in the world?

This means before you go and jump into the water head first creating another blog website, you have to understand the reason why you are doing it. Make it purposeful.

For me, the reason was not clearly defined at the beginning. I was doing it as a fun hobby on weekends since I was a teenager. As things evolved I did it primarily for the income to help pay for college.

The blog gave me a huge benefit because it allowed me to pursue my studies by giving me the time freedom and flexibility to study in addition to the income to pursue those studies.

In the end, I got lucky with the benefits because I had no clue what I was getting into.

Before I started my blog, I'd never read a book about blogging. In fact, there were no books on the subject back then. Now I see hundreds of blogging books and blog websites, but few with a clear and defined plan. That is the reason why I decided to write this book.

Based on your situation you need to decide why it is you want to blog.

You can do it for income, time freedom, passion, location flexibility, or another reason - but know your "why" because when things get difficult, you will know your purpose and what you are looking to accomplish.

Reason #1: Income

Blogging for income is one of the main reasons people decide to start a blog.

Blogging has low barriers to entry as it only costs a few hundred dollars to start and you can do it part-time while you are working a full-time job.

If income is your reason, then you clearly have defined your reason.

One caveat for some people is that it does take time to build a blog that starts generating income.

This means if you are looking for quick riches then blogging is not the path to take.

On the other hand, as you build things you can generate a great income source.

You might be wondering how great?

It depends on the blog, niche, products, customer base, and many other factors.

You have some blogs that make no money and others that make more than $1,000,000 per year!

Unfortunately, money does not come quickly with a blog business. It takes a great deal of time and energy to build a profitable blog, but you can do it if you put the hard work, time, and dedication into it.

I will give you some financial insights later.

However, you will never be successful at creating a blog business if you don't have the other parts of the business that matter and that's what I will share with you in this book.

Reason #2: Passion

Passion is another reason many people begin to blog.

I believe passion is important in many aspects of life so that you can stick with the subject or topic for the long-term. One of the beauties behind blogging is that you can choose your subject matter or topic.

It is difficult to say if you are passionate blogging if you have never blogged before. Even if you have written some content online – having a successful online business and writing a few articles or posts online are two different things.

I think in this instance many people refer to the passion as the subject matter that they write about or the act of writing itself.

Getting back to passion, if you understand that blogging is not a one-month business to quick riches then your ability to stay with it will be easier – especially if you have the passion.

From personal insight, I have seen many bloggers quit early. They often quit right before things start accelerating or picking up. This is why I recommend you plan at least a minimum of one-year commitment until your blog starts to generate revenue.

Here is an example of how blog traffic (or sales) grows on a website and a few common quitting spots for people. Most people typically quit right before things have a chance to build to the upside.

An example of sales or traffic for a business can be shown in the graph below along with where people quit. Often times most people quit right before things take off or power higher.

Another quit point right before growth takes off again

Quit point

The same is true if you are starting a brick-and-mortar business.

At the beginning you have investment capital that you may need to pay off or general expenses. It takes time for the energy to build, the traffic sources to kick in, the customers to get to know you, and time for them to build a relationship with you.

The same is true with a blog business. It takes a handful of months to get things moving. You'll have to learn the ins and outs of online business.

If you are new to making money online you will have to learn marketing concepts, play with strategies, but most importantly you have to continue making improvements and testing to see what works.

That is why I say give a minimum of one year until you start generating profits.

Although none of that is important if you can't stick with the topic and passion helps fuel that drive.

Reason #3: Time freedom

Time freedom is another huge bonus that many blog business owners enjoy.

For me this was exceptionally important when I started my diamond blog. It was imperative that I had the time freedom so that I could continue studying at University.

If time freedom is important to you, then blogging could be a great way to have more time flexibility.

I am not saying you won't have to work, but I am saying you can work the hours you want to work whether that's at 10 AM on a Sunday or at midnight on a Wednesday.

Unfortunately, time freedom and flexibility will not happen overnight. It will only happen once you have a few critical pieces of your blog business setup correctly.

At the beginning when you are starting your blog there is going to be an enormous amount of work. For example, you will have to get the domain name, purchase web hosting, setup a website, brainstorm about products, create content, marketing strategies, and the list goes on.

Once you have these things set up and a system in place to help you manage the workflow, then you may be able to run on autopilot. This means you can create content in advance and have them scheduled to release sometime in the future.

For example, on my stock trading blog (http://www.tradersfly.com) and business blog (http://www.backstageincome.com) I usually create evergreen content which has no time-sensitivity.

Evergreen content is content that can be created at any time for the future and released at any time. This means rather than creating a content piece of what is happening in the business world today or what company is releasing a new product, I may create a content piece about marketing tips or how to setup an advertising campaign.

In the end, by creating evergreen content it allows me to create 5, 10, 20, or 30 videos in a weekend and then my work is done for half the year as far as blog content goes.

If I want to do a special post a certain week then I can pop it in there and shift everything else forward. The rest of the time I can trade stocks, read, attend seminars, go to yoga class, write books, create products, spend time with my family, or travel. I am an educational junkie, so I like these things, but that's what I want to do.

What do you want to do and get from your blog? That's the more important question. This will drive your motivation and work ethic to keep your blog thriving. If your blog business can help you meet your end goal, you're more inclined to continue to push through the difficult challenges that lie ahead.

The initial stage is difficult to get past. Most people don't make it because getting started is difficult. You are moving against gravity similar to a spaceship blasting off. You need a lot of rocket fuel to get off the ground as you need to build up that energy.

On the bright side, once you get through it, you can have a blog business that works on autopilot.

When you have flexibility with your time, you can spend more time with your kids, contribute to your community, play music, or anything else your heart desires.

Reason #4: Location Flexibility

If you are someone who enjoys traveling around the world then you would enjoy the location flexibility a blog business can offer you.

The flexibility of being able to travel the world is something that one may not be able to put a price tag on.

For some people, this benefit will not be that important, but for others it will be a gold-mine!

Of course, you would have to set up the blog so that it allowed for location flexibility. Meaning, if you are ordering products to do product reviews, it would be more difficult to do this if you did not have a fixed location. So you would have to think about your content and products and the way that you manage the business aspects.

However that is not to say that it is not possible. You just have to plan for that. It is definitely easier to have location flexibility with a blog business than a corporation or a brick and mortar business.

In the end, it is important to know why you are getting into the blog business. If you know clearly the reasons, you will have a vision of what to shoot for. Choose a goal to shoot for and laser focus on that goal.

CHAPTER 3:
HOW MUCH DOES IT COST TO START A BLOG?

If you've already decided that you want to start a blog business and that it's a great fit for you then you might be wondering how much does it cost to start?

As with any business there will be costs associated with starting a blog business. Along with your time and energy, which I believe are the biggest cost because you can't buy more time, there will be financial costs.

Additional resources, tools, and services that you may need to get your blog started below can be found at http://www.backstageincome.com/resources/

Here are some of those tools and services that you are going to need along with approximately how much you should expect to pay for them:

Web hosting ($10 to $25 per month)

Web hosting is the computer (server) that keeps your website online 24 hours a day, 7 days a week and allows people to access it.

As your blog receives more traffic, you may need to upgrade your web hosting. If you have an extremely popular blog this could be a few hundred dollars per month.

Although this means you would be receiving a massive amount of traffic and probably a good amount of revenue.

Domain name ($10 to $50 per year)

The domain name is where your blog lives. Think of it as your address like yourname.com, forbes.com, facebook.com, etc.

I purchase my domain names at GoDaddy.

Depending on the domain extension such yourname.com, .net, .guru, .expert or many other extensions. Some extensions cost upward of $1,000 as some countries have reserved certain extensions.

However a common dot com can cost you as little as $10 to $50 per year if you get creative and find one that is not taken along with depending on the privacy settings you select.

If you want more privacy then you can pay a little extra to have it private such as $20 extra per year. This means people can't back-check your personal information by looking at your domain name registration details.

Another way to avoid this privacy issue is to get a P.O. Box with your local post office which may solve other issues once you start shipping items and have a return label.

Designer or programmer ($200 to $1,000)

If you need someone to help you set up your blog then it may be worth it to pay someone to do the setup work.

Often times it's great to hire a student or someone on a freelancing website like upwork.com or freelancer.com as it may save you some money when you are first getting started.

Rookie Mistake: Blowing most of your money on a fancy theme or website. The initial goal is about getting the right foundation in terms of content and putting out value to your audience. The look of your website is not a top priority no matter what a designer or developer tells you.

Content writers (price varies)

Depending on your blog and how you set it up, you may want to hire people that will help you do some writing. If you don't think you can keep up with creating the content yourself or if you plan to build an authority blog business with many authors then you may need to budget for content creators accordingly.

Some content pieces can cost as little as $5 dollars or as high as a few hundred dollars depending on the quality, subject matter and the writer.

You can save a lot of money if you get international writers – some blog posts may only cost $5. Writers in the USA for the same length of content may cost $25 per post or more!

Just remember you will often get what you pay for.

International writers may be cheaper, but the language skills may not be up to par. USA or Canadian based writers may be a bit more expensive, but they often have better English skills.

Video, photo, or other equipment ($100 to $1,000)

If your blog is photo or video oriented and you don't have the equipment, then you may need to purchase video or photo equipment such as a tripod, camera, lights, and background paper.

To save some cash or initial startup money, you could use your smart phone and tape it to a cardboard box creating a do-it-yourself stability stand that could act as a tripod, but if you want some decent equipment you may need to spend a few dollars.

I find food and travel blogs have a healthy amount of a photos and videos. This means you should plan your equipment needs accordingly based on your industry as well as how you can make your content better.

Software ($100 to $500)

Depending on the blog or how you want to create content, you may want to purchase some software that helps your workflow.

This could include photo editing software to help you adjust your pictures, accounting software, or it may include a headset, microphone, and Dragon NaturallySpeaking that types for you as you speak into the microphone.

I find that Dragon NaturallySpeaking saves me countless hours each year when I do longer form content.

In fact, the majority of this book was written simply by speaking and using the software.

Online services ($15 to $100 per month)

Beyond the main critical requirements like web hosting and a domain name, you may need to have some subscriptions to a few services such as Aweber to manage your mailing list.

There may be other subscription services that come across your desk and catch your attention, but most are not as critical as a mailing list service and often a distraction.

I see that all too often many people get sucked into subscription services at the beginning like an accounting software, to-do list manager, sales tracker, analytics, form or lead building software, and so many others. If you are just getting started don't get sucked into the trap!

This is one of the reasons many online business owners fail. They pay hundreds of dollars a month at the beginning and focus on the shiny objects when they should be focused on product building, marketing, and customers.

Rookie Mistake: Spending too much money on shiny objects or online tools that are not necessary – especially at the beginning.

Focus on things that actually grow and build your business – not things that manage your business.

For your accounting, you could file some papers in a notebook and do it the old fashioned way. If you need a to-do list manager, use index cards. To discuss a project with a service provider don't be scared to use your phone and actually talk on the phone rather than subscribing to a monthly service software package. You don't need the fancy stuff at the beginning when you are still trying to stand up on your feet.

The fact is, if you are using various software when you are getting started, you will spend a large amount of time just figuring out the software in the system when there are more critical things that need to be completed.

Keep these subscription services at a minimal!

If you are still attracted to the technology and the shiny objects, here are some alternatives to get you started to crave those needs and to keep your costs low:

Book keeping and accounting: Use Evernote or Waveaccounting.com. They are free for most basic uses. Evernote is $50 a year for a premium membership. Compare this to Quickbooks online at $120 a year or Xero. Stick to basics.

When you are making more money and have so many transactions that you have a hard time keeping up with that is a good problem to have. At this point can upgrade your accounting software.

Task manager and working in teams: Trello is one of my favorite tools along with Asana.com. Both tools are free for just a few team members to work together.

Social media manager: Not really necessary in my opinion, but people preach it. If anything use bufferapp.com as it's free for basic use and $10 a month for the premium version. Hootsuite is also quite good depending on your needs and relatively inexpensive.

Merchant account: PayPal or Square. Low fees to get started and no need to deal with crazy contracts. Keeps things really simple in the big scheme of things.

File storage: You can use your web hosting company but if you need some more space Google Drive is quite cost effective and cheaper than Dropbox from what I've found.

Overall if you watch your costs, your total expenses for starting a blog business are relatively minimal compared to starting a brick-and-mortar business.

Here is a rough ballpark figure of what you can expect to pay to get your blog off the ground. Note this does not include any advertising, traffic tools, or other bells and shiny objects that you may be attracted to purchase.

Item	Cost
Web hosting	$120
Domain name	$15
Designer	$500
Content	$300
Equipment	$500
Software	$200
Services	$200
Total Yearly Cost (Estimated)	$1,835

CHAPTER 4:
WHY MOST BLOGGERS FAIL

Failure is inevitable and you will fail throughout your life, but if you learn to improve and continue moving forward you will get better.

If you want to have a successful blog you need to know why most blogger's fail. Knowing what it takes and what is necessary for success will make your blogging business path easier and more profitable.

There are two main things that you need in order to have a successful blog. Those things are the inner game and outer game.

The first main reason bloggers fail is because of their lack of the **outer game**. The outer game concepts are the external things that need to be done that most people think of.

Think of the outer game as setting up the blog, using technology, and getting around the web using certain tools.

The second reason most bloggers fail is the **inner game**. The inner game is about mastering your human psychology and behavior. This includes your focus, discipline, attitude, or the ability to adjust quickly when something isn't working as you expect it to.

Think of the inner game as the internal things inside of you that affect your actions.

Insight: Over the years I have seen many people fail. Most people fail not because they don't know what to do, but because they don't do the right things. The failure often comes from lack of the inner game. This might be lack of consistency, focus, not changing paths when necessary, etc. If you can master your own inner game it will give you an advantage to where many people fail.

Treating your business like a business

The fact is that most people who start their blog business don't recognize it as a "business" – so they don't treat it like a business. Many think of it as a place to post their vacation photos, their baby pictures, or about their personal life. They rarely think about their visitors and future customers.

When you are blogging there should be a purpose and goal.

You should be adding value to people's lives whether that's teaching them something new, entertaining them, socializing with them, or inspiring them.

There are also many bloggers who create blogs that are identical to other blogs on the internet with a slightly different spin on the content.

Often times, the content is regurgitated, not specific, and much of the information is fluff because they put minimal effort, and expect quick results.

I've seen this happen when blog owners hire international writers to write quick articles, but many times these articles are 500 or 1000 words, are fairly basic, and feel like vanilla without a deeper substance.

Thinking long-term

Their content consists of random topics that don't build to future products. They rarely see the long-term goal of what they are trying to build, nor do they see the future products that they will offer.

Before I started my http://www.backstageincome.com business blog I planned my list of future products. This included a minimum of 10 products at different price points and levels.

You have to have a plan!

Without a plan you won't get anywhere whether that's a blog business or in other areas of life.

If you don't know where you want to go, it will be difficult to figure out which roads to take. Once you narrow down where your destination is – you'll be able to figure out the right paths to take.

That is why I emphasized earlier know the reason behind knowing why you want to start a blog business.

CHAPTER 5:
BUILDING YOUR BLOG EMPIRE

Many think of gold riches, things they can buy, and a future lifestyle as they daydream about their future blog business. They think of it becoming huge and you *can* make it huge, but there is a specific approach to creating an empire.

Keep in mind that this is a business and you should always think of it in terms of a business. If you don't think about it that way, then it will be a hobby and one that never grow to anything worthwhile.

If you want your blog to be a massive blog in terms of traffic, customers, and profits, you need focus on creating an authority blog.

What do I mean by authority blog?

An authority blog is a blog that has many contributors to the content and many people writing, creating videos, and managing the tasks to help fuel the blog.

You've probably run across many authority blogs before, but you may have not thought of them as blogs. Some of these blogs disguise themselves as standard big websites such as:

- ★ Huffingtonpost.com (World news)
- ★ TMZ.com (celebrity news and gossip)
- ★ Mashable.com (Tech and Social Media)
- ★ Lifehacker.com (Life hacks and time saving tips)

- ★ Engadget.com (Tech and gear)
- ★ Stylemepretty.com (Weddings)

If you want your blog business to be huge, this is the route to go because there is no way that you as an individual can produce high-quality content every single day, three or more times per day and still run the other parts of the business. It may be possible, but you wouldn't have a lifestyle that you enjoy.

To have a blog business that's an empire, then you must have a vision of creating an authority blog!

Normally, an authority blog starts with one author or as an independent blog and eventually grows into an authority blog. What you don't want to do at the beginning is to start hiring 100 authors from the moment you buy your domain because the financial capital that is required to do that is high.

Not to mention, blog growth can be slow if you don't know what you are doing or if it's your first time starting a blog. For this reason, you want to minimize the cost of your mistakes (and you will have them).

This means you don't need to publish five times per week on a new website nor do you need to hire 50 writers the first week your blog is launched.

Start slow and post once a week for a few months then you can increase it to two or three posts per week. After six months or a year you can increase it again to posting daily if you like.

The time line is not important. Increase things gradually so you keep a good consistent flow for your audience.

On the other hand, if you want to keep things small, do not care to have an authority blog, don't want to worry about other people posting, or don't want to manage authors and contributors then you can still be successful with a blog that you personally manage and handle on your own.

You may eventually need help with doing administrative tasks if the blog becomes popular, but these things could be outsourced to a virtual assistant or a small team depending on your needs.

In either case, look at the bigger picture!

Do you want a major authority blog business or are you looking to do this as a personal venture?

Have a plan based on your initial goal and what you want out of the blog business.

Authority Blog vs. Independent Blog

Depending on whether you want to become an authority blog or stay an independent blog, each avenue has advantages and disadvantages.

Now this isn't to say that you can't change your path from an independent blog to an authority blog once things get going (which is typically how authority blogs are formed).

However, sometimes knowing your long-term goals will serve you better because you can plan accordingly based on your future vision.

Here are some of the advantages and disadvantages of the different business blog models.

Item	Authority	Independent
Startup time / costs	High	Lower
Competition	High	Often Lower
People required	Many	Less
Income potential	Higher	Often Less
Your time required once things are moving	Less	Still requires your time

When looking at this comparison chart keep in mind that not all things are as linear as they seem. For example, the income potential may be higher on a per-person basis (for you) on an independent blog than an authority blog because the costs and fees to run an authority blog may be expensive if you don't know how to manage your cash-flow properly.

Always think about things deeper than just what the chart says. It is only provided to give you an opportunity to weigh your options.

For example, think about the competition that is involved. If you want to start an authority website that discusses news, politics, tech, and business all under one blog you have multiple other blogs that are competing for your customer or visitor's reading time.

On the business side you may have Forbes.com. On the tech side you may have engadget.com. You will have an overwhelming amount of competitors if you try to tackle topics that are too broad too quickly.

This is why most of the time (especially in the beginning) it is best to start small with an independent blog and then later develop it into an authority blog if that's where you want to go.

Always think of the bigger picture of what you want and plan for it.

Sometimes the best businesses are not ones that dominate broad areas, but dominate specific niches where people are hungry for a solution!

Rookie Mistake: Trying to start too big of a website too quickly. Focus on a specific niche that you can dominate and then grow it or expand it once you see your concepts work.

CHAPTER 6:
THE ANATOMY OF A SUCCESSFUL BLOG BUSINESS

By now you might be getting the hang of understanding the blog business and what it's all about. However you might be wondering what is the blueprint to make it successful and how does it all work.

Here is a diagram and breakdown to give you a visual.

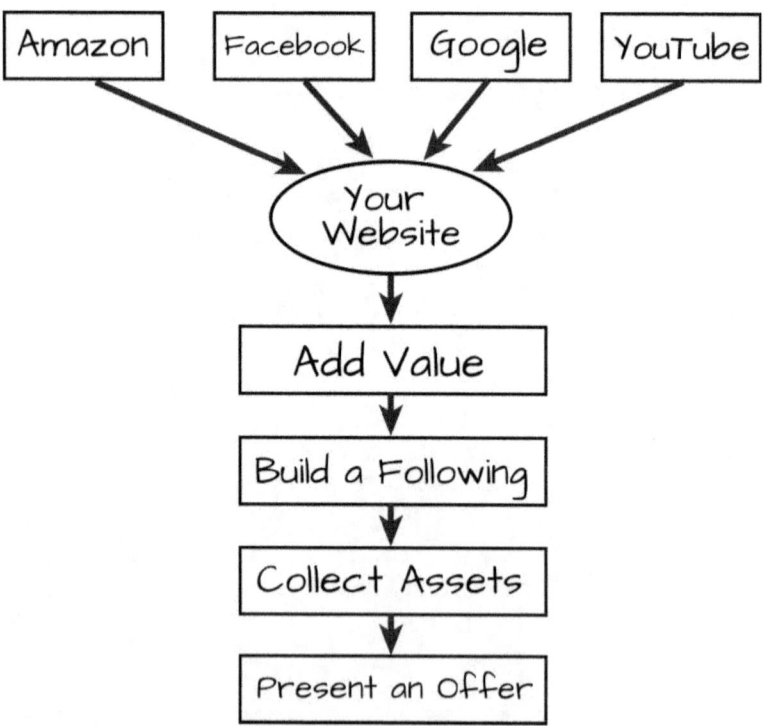

In this diagram I wanted to show you exactly how the process works. This is a simple version of how everything works together to help you create a blog business that's profitable – but if you wanted the blueprints, that is the simplified blueprint.

I will give you an overview of each of these steps, but to go into depth of each step would be beyond the scope of this book.

In fact, I could write a whole book on each one of the steps, as they require a deeper study. For example, in the first step when you move people from authority websites there are dozens of books on traffic generation, advertising, and search engine marketing. For the last step when you present an offer there are books, seminars, and video courses on selling, conversion, writing killer offers, and copywriting.

However, I think if you have a solid foundation in understanding the overall concept it will point you in the right direction.

The overall process goes something like this:

1. Redirect traffic to your blog from authority websites
2. When a user visits your blog, you add value to their life
3. Build a relationship with your audience
4. Collect an asset (such as an email address)
5. Make an offer for a product or service
6. Continue to add value & create offers for products and services

Some of these sequences can be shifted and changed and you may have steps in between. Here is an example of that. Notice the differences and the sub-steps. You can have an infinite amount of sub-steps for each step.

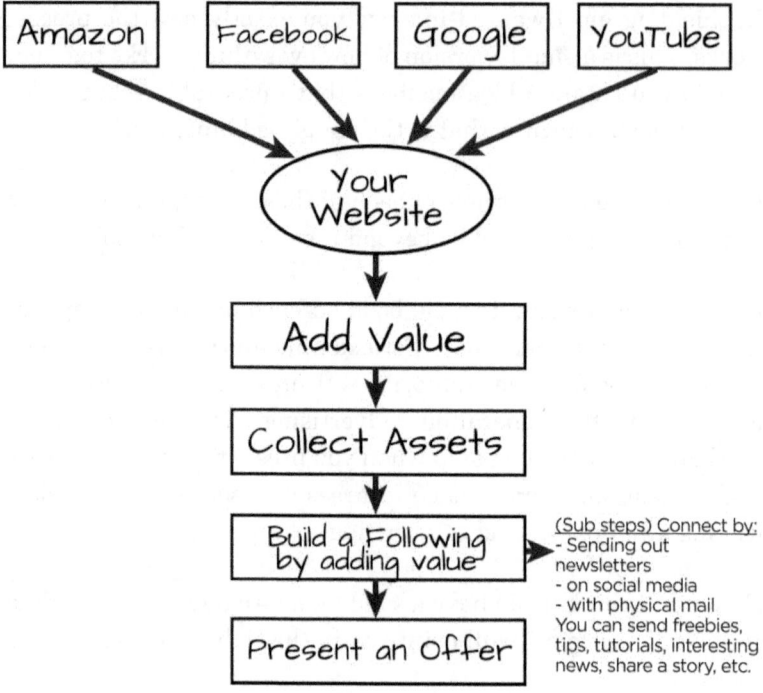

You should also notice we switched collect assets and build a following in the sequence. In theory a few of these can be swapped. There is no exact way to grill. There are variations according to taste. Some people may marinate and others may glaze at the end. It is all about figuring out what works for you, your niche, and your audience.

The goal is that you need to give enough value before someone gives you their phone number or their contact details (an asset) and you also need to give enough value before you present an offer.

This means there may be more steps, sub-steps, and sequences between each step depending on the product and customer.

A more expensive product for example takes more time to purchase because the risks are higher. Keep these things in your mind as we go in detail for each step.

This is similar to buying a house vs buying a pack of gum. Gum is an impulse buy because it is on the shelf and ready for the taking. It also costs much less. When you buy a house you need to think about it more, there is more paperwork that goes with it, and the price is higher than a pack of gum.

This means if your products price is higher than average keep it in mind that your prospects purchase time frame may be longer.

1. Redirecting traffic:

The first step to making a blog business work is to bring traffic to your blog.

You can do this with search engines, advertising, social media, viral videos, billboards, networking, and the list goes on. The strategies are endless and they change over time.

Different strategies will work better for different niches. For example, social media may work great for a younger demographic, but terrible for assisted living products. This means you will have to test different strategies to find what works best for your niche and how to best connect with your audience.

As far as bringing in traffic goes, you are redirecting traffic to your blog. People (the traffic) are already online - the only thing you are doing is getting them to visit your blog website. (The people who truly generate online traffic are the Internet and cable providers).

The best way to redirect traffic to your website is to go to the biggest traffic players on the Internet. Meaning, go to the authority websites and see how you can pull their traffic to your blog.

This step is about getting the eye balls to your website, so where are there more eyes currently? The big websites. So this means you have to pull people from the popular websites (authority websites) to *your* website.

This could be in the form of placing advertisements, writing guest posts on authority blogs, posting ads on craigslist, adding products on Amazon, or listing products on eBay with your YouTube videos inside the listing to help bring exposure to your products or content.

Your goal at this stage is to get people from the largest websites to your blog.

Visit Alexa.com for a list of top 500 visited websites. You won't be able to use every website to redirect traffic, but it may give you a few ideas. You only need one or two big players to get some great traffic.

Each authority website that you aim to pull traffic from will require a different technique. For example, to get traffic from YouTube you will need to make videos. To get traffic from Amazon, you need to have a product such as a book. This means if you don't have one – you will need to write one to get exposure from Amazon.

Rookie Mistake: Trying to dominate multiple authority websites at once. Instead focus on creating a popular presence on one and then expanding and moving on to the next one. Juggling five things at once is difficult.

As far as techniques go, there are numerous marketing tactics that you may have heard of such as adding your link in your emails, commenting on other blogs, or adding your signature in forums. However, rather than focusing 80% of your energy to get that 20% of the traffic – focus your energy on the big authority websites to get 80% of your traffic from them.

2. Add Value

Once people are on your website and come to your blog you need to add value to their life.

Depending on the niche that you are in there are different ways to add value.

For example, if you run a photography service business you could give them a training video on "How to hire the best photographer for your wedding."

If you are a personal chef or sell cookbooks, then you could create videos and recipes that people would enjoy looking at, getting inspiration from, or creating themselves.

If you're great at applying makeup, then you could show others how to properly apply makeup to different skin tones or which products are the best to use to achieve various results.

There are different ways to add value to people online. You have to figure out which way works best for your niche.

In the big picture, the Internet is about content. Whether you're making tutorials, creating music, speaking, broadcasting news, entertaining, writing books, giving tips, or pointing people in the right direction. All of these methods work and add value to people in different ways.

The key is to find what your customer wants and needs and then give it to them.

3. Build a Following

As you continue to create content and add value to your audience you then start to build a loyal following. This step sometimes happens after you collect the asset, as we want to collect an asset as quickly as possible. However, sometimes relationships take time to cultivate and for this reason, you may need to build a following before you acquire an asset.

To build a following takes time similar to a crockpot cooking. For some niches this will take longer than others.

For example, it may take longer for someone to trust you on sensitive topics such as dealing with alcohol or dating advice because people may be more skeptical than if you are showing people how to weave and cross-stitch.

One way to build trust and rapport is to share personal details and stories with your audience. You have to build trust if you ever plan to sell to your customers in the future.

Think of why is it that you go to eat at a restaurant.

It might be the selection, taste, decor, but in the end it comes down to trust.

Would you eat at a restaurant where you don't trust that the food is safe to eat? Of course not! The core of it all comes down to trust.

Building a following and trust takes time. Trust is earned. The great news is once you earn your visitor's trust you can help them improve their life and they will reward you for it.

4. Collecting Assets

Once you've built trust and rapport with your audience you need to acquire an asset. Getting an asset is one of the most important things that you can do.

If you can start this process sooner such as the moment people get to your website or blog – then do so. Although, sometimes it takes time to get to this point so you have to add value and build trust before you can acquire the asset.

Rookie Mistake: Not building your customer list soon enough. The longer you wait on building your customer or email list the more time is wasted and potential customers lost! Start building your email list the day your website is live!

In simple terms an asset is the contact information to your prospect or potential customer. It is information that you can use to connect with your customer at some point in the future at any time.

We all surf the web anonymously. We can go on a website, look at it for a few seconds, and then sign off or go to the next website.

The downside to this for a business online is that you never get to know your blog visitors or who they are, nor can you reach them if you want to get a hold of them unless you have their contact details.

In the marketing world we call the information that we acquire "the asset."

In the online space the asset is usually referring to the email address. However there are multiple levels of an asset.

Collecting email addresses is a start. As your relationship develops with your customers and they purchase from you, you may have an asset list that includes customer's home addresses and telephone numbers. I would consider these assets to be more valuable because you are able to connect with them in a more personal way.

Think of it this way – how many emails do you get each day? Maybe 20, 50, 100, or 1,000 if you're a bit more popular?

Now how many packages or post cards do you get in the mail each day? Maybe 3 or 5 a week if you are lucky?

The more personal you can get, the deeper the relationship. The end result is they trust you more, which means in the future when you present product offers and services to your list of prospects they have a higher probability of purchasing.

To sum up, at the bare minimum, you want to start collecting email addresses to build a quality potential customer list.

You can use Aweber and start sending out an email newsletter at least once every few weeks to maintain a relationship with your audience.

If you are interested in signing up to Aweber I would appreciate it if you used my affiliate link: http://www.aweber.com/?397816

This doesn't cost you anything extra by using the link, but it gives me a small little credit to my account when you sign up.

Once you have a newsletter, this means that every week or two you are sending out free tips, product reviews, insights, and ways to help them contribute to your audience as well as build a relationship.

If you can get closer to your audience and acquire a physical address, whether that's by selling them an e-book, or giving away stuff for the price of shipping, then you will be ahead of your competition.

5. Presenting the offer

After you've built a relationship through the newsletter you can now present an offer for a product or service.

By presenting an offer you are giving something of high value that your audience will love! Of course the product or service should be related to your blog.

For example, if you are a personal chef and you run a blog that includes a variety of great professional recipe, then what you may do is present an offer for great cookbooks for other people that are interested in learning how to cook like you.

When you present these cookbooks you can be an affiliate and get a commission for each sale you bring the author. You can do this simply through Amazon or just search for "affiliate networks" online and a dozens of them will come up.

If you have your own book or your own product, then you can present that offer to your newsletter members as well. Often times you will make more from your own products than just getting a commission from other people's products and that is just simply because the margins are in your favor.

Now you may need to do more work when it is your own products such as shipping or customer relationship management, but nevertheless the income potential is a bit higher.

If you have a service-oriented business such as a dance studio or martial arts classes, then you might present an offer in your newsletter such as "try our classes for free for 3 weeks and get two free private lessons when you sign up before August 15th."

This type of offer might be great for newsletters that are focused on targeting a local audience. If the majority of your income is made through personal interaction, then you will need to focus on offers that can get people to your physical location.

There are virtually unlimited amount of offers that you can present to your prospects. The only limit is your creativity. However, one thing you don't want to do is constantly promote offers week after week as this will seem pushy and not genuine.

Keep a balance between adding value to your prospect through your blog and newsletter and presenting your prospects with offers.

Not everyone is looking to purchase right at this moment. Some people like to shop around for weeks or months before they pull the buy trigger.

6. Rinse and Repeat

Your final step is to rinse and repeat the process if it's working. If things are not working properly at any one stage you make adjustments.

This means that you should continue to add value to your prospects and promote products, services, and offers that you believe would be of high value to your audience.

You can't do this without having their contact information and you can't get their contact information if you don't get the traffic.

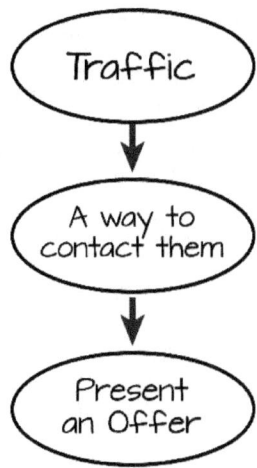

All the steps work together with synergy.

You need each step to get to the next step so the process can continue.

If you look at this from a bigger picture, it's about building a relationship slowly.

That's what any business or exchange of money is about – it's about exchanging value from one person to the other.

CHAPTER 8:
WHERE DOES THE MONEY COME FROM?

It costs money to keep a blog business alive. Capital is what fuels any business.

The important question is where does money come from for your blog business?

There are three ways to make money online:

1. Sell your own products
2. Sell someone else's product
3. Sponsorship (this can be pay for clicks or pay for views)

3 Primary Ways to Make Money Online

Each method alone to bring in revenue can be strong, but combining multiple income streams is even more powerful. It also reduces your risk if you have multiple income streams.

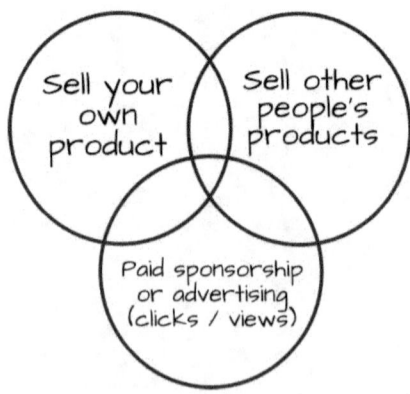

* Often times the industry uses the acronyms CPM for cost per thousand for views and CPC for cost per click. However sponsorship may refer to mentioning a product or company in a blog post, video, or podcast.

We mentioned these things earlier in the hierarchy of the income streams. However in this example I want to show it to you in a different way.

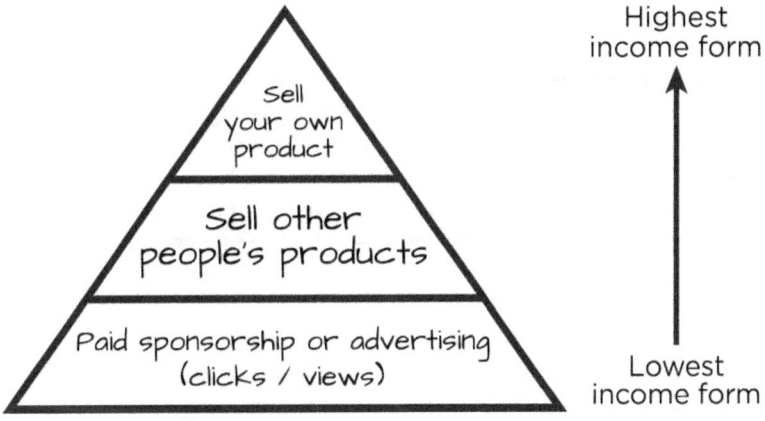

Your own product

You will often make the most money from selling your own products so long as you can sell and move the products. You will make less money from being an affiliate and even less from pay per click advertising assuming all other things are equal.

Does that mean it's impossible to make a living from clicks and advertisements? No, but you will need more clicks and traffic to make a similar amount if you had a few hundred loyal customers and you are selling a product.

If you've studied the product pipelines above, then you get an idea that it's very beneficial to have your own product. By having your own product you have the highest margin and most flexibility.

Unfortunately, the downside is that not everyone can create a product. It is one of the more difficult ways to make money because it takes a lot of time, knowledge, and skillsets, especially if you never made a product before, but it can be one of the most rewarding.

Side note: Rewards or added benefits from creating your products are not always monetary based. Often times the rewards are intrinsic. For example, if you have your own book you can use it as leverage to get speaking gigs and build credibility to get your foot in the door.

Your own products can be anything you can think of that relates to your niche and audience. For example you can manufacture a helpful tool with plastic injection molding for the kitchen or you can create an informational product such as a book or video course.

If you have a loyal audience and you have a way to add value on a consistent basis then you can set up a continuity program.

This is something people pay for to get access each month. It can be something they get in the mail each month (like a magazine or a surprise gift box).

The sky is the limit!

You never want to force a membership down someone's throat, but if you have a monthly residual income with a continuity program then you have stability.

You can see an example of my recurring membership program at
http://tradersfly.com/plans/

Selling someone else's product (affiliates)

The middle road would be to sell someone else's product. This is where you become an affiliate.

As an affiliate you can earn anywhere from 1% to 100% of the sale depending on the product.

You might be thinking why would they give you 100% of the sale?

Well remember the concept of getting the asset. If you are bringing people to the vendor and selling their product they are acquiring a customer. This would give them an opportunity to sell to these customers in the future.

This means that they have other backend products or other offers they can promote to these new customers either through an upsell or a down sell (offering something of higher or lower value).

You might be wondering then how does this affiliate process work?

Let's say you are doing camera reviews and at the bottom of your review (or at the end of your video) you say "click here to purchase this camera." If the visitor clicks your link and purchases the camera then you would make a healthy commission from that sale.

As an example, if the product was a DSLR camera for $1,950 you may make anywhere between $50 and $500 or more depending on the terms as different affiliates pay different commission rates.

That's pretty cool for doing a review right?

Now the alarms in your brain may be ringing and you probably understand why many people do product reviews!

Paid Sponsorships, Ads, CPC, and CPM

Paid sponsorship is usually the easiest form of making money online because you are selling advertising space on your website.

It is usually the fastest way to make your first dollar from your website if you've never made any money from your website before.

By ad space, I don't only mean banner space on your website. You can actually get paid for mentioning someone's product in your YouTube videos or in your newsletters however this usually comes later once you have a following or a sustainable traffic base.

There are many different forms of sponsorships. Of course CPM, CPC, and banner ads on your website is the easiest and most popular method to get some kind of revenue stream. The downside is that it's usually not as rewarding especially if you have minimal traffic.

The more traffic that you have the more exposure you can bring to brands, companies, and products that one exposure. In essence that is what sponsorship is all about.

It is about bringing exposure to someone's brand, product, and getting them the eyeballs or the sales so that you can get paid for the exposure or take a cut of the profits.

You can create all kinds of sponsorship campaigns such as mentioning a product in one of your videos, talking about a website in your podcast, sending out a tweet, or sending a suggested product to your newsletter.

You can get very creative with sponsorships and it is only limited based on how creative you get.

Just keep in mind that often times you are sending traffic to another website when you're promoting them which in theory you are getting rid of the people looking at your website (at least temporarily).

In addition, if you don't have a lot of traffic or do not have a website with some authority then your sponsorship rates and revenues may be minimal.

Rookie Mistake: Focusing only on one revenue model specifically PPC or banner ads because of its ease to set up. Always continue to improve and think of what is the next step. Revenue is generated when you add value to people.

Summary on revenue

After reading about the product pipeline I think by now you understand that you should have a product or service or at least plan to have one soon.

Even if you don't have your own products to start, you can promote someone else's product for a commission.

One tip regarding affiliate products: do not constantly promote by pushing and pumping the sale. It will be noticeable and you will lose respect from your audience.

Only promote products that you truly believe in because your reputation is at stake. If you promote products strictly to make a few bucks and things don't go as planned eventually your credibility will be at risk.

I enjoy promoting affiliate products myself and you can take a look at my list and how I do it at:
http://www.backstageincome.com/resources/

On this page whenever someone clicks and purchases any of the services or products then I will receive a percentage of that sale. It doesn't cost any extra for my customer to purchase or sign-up to any of the products or services. I simply get a commission for promoting the company or the service.

Final note on advertising revenue

I want to be clear that I'm not against selling ad space or ad revenue on your blog. I think it's fantastic for people that have a great amount of traffic!

Unfortunately, for most people this is not a viable income stream and it's one of the lowest forms of payment that you can get. One of the reasons is that you're not building an audience and you're not building customers.

In fact, you are pushing customers away from your website to other products and services that other companies are providing. If people are going to other websites that means they are spending less time on your website.

I believe that beginners who are starting their first online business get sucked into the advertising method because after all, it is the easiest method to use to start making money online. All one really needs to do is to copy and paste some code and the ads are live whereas to create your own product there are many more steps and a lot more work involved.

As far as ad payouts are concerned, different niches will give you different payout percentages and amounts. For example it costs more to advertise an insurance company because of competition than it does for a roofing company. This means if you are blogging in a highly expensive niche then the payout can be nice for the ad revenue especially if your website gets great traffic.

Here are some industries that pay higher in ad revenue:

* ★ insurance
* ★ loans
* ★ attorney and lawyers
* ★ credit (such as credit cards and credit checks)
* ★ hosting
* ★ investing
* ★ stock trading
* ★ rehabilitation and treatment
* ★ gas and electricity
* ★ software

The downside is that some of these industries and niches may not be that interesting to talk about, but they are lucrative, highly competitive, and money generating businesses.

In addition, always check the affiliates or products availability. What I mean by this is you can't offer a service like being a lawyer overnight to your website visitors. The expansion possibilities have limits.

There are rules and regulations and not many affiliate programs for these industries. However for things like web hosting and credit cards there are tons of affiliates.

CHAPTER 7:
THE PRODUCT PIPELINE

When I first heard the frustration my audience had with the blogging books available, I decided to pick up a few books and see for myself. I quickly noticed the gap in what authors shared versus what one had to do to make a successful blog business.

I found in many books, authors focused on looking at the primary source of revenue from advertisements such as Google Adsense. Unfortunately, this is one of the lowest forms of income online.

Here is the income forms visually designed in a hierarchy form that we discussed earlier:

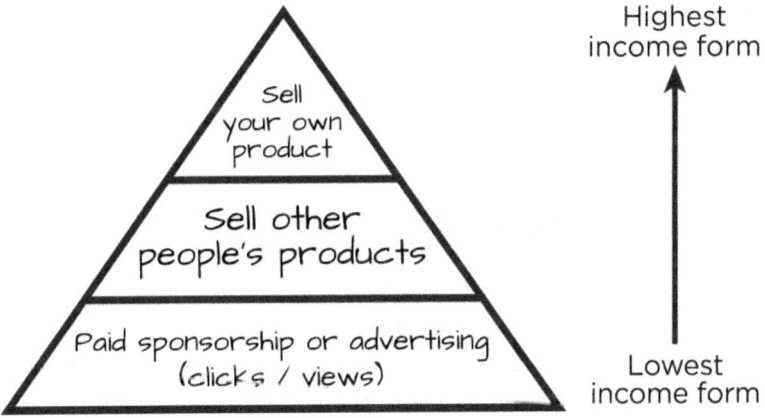

Let me enlighten the revenue concept for you.

Stay away from ad revenue as much as possible at the beginning because it is a trap for new online business owners!

It will be one of your worst forms of revenue unless your blog is getting a few hundred thousand to a million hits per year. Instead, focus on creating a product pipeline that your prospects can go through after you add value to their lives.

Not to mention, if you place ads for other products and services, your visitors may be moving away from your blog or website. Isn't this the opposite of what you want? You want people to stay as long as possible on your website.

In either case, would you rather have 500,000 people that you have to please or 500 loyal customers that will purchase every single thing that you showed to them?

I believe that it is easier to keep 500 people happy than 500,000 people.

Keep in mind, your prospects will go through your product pipeline after you've gathered an email address or their mailing address. For some people it will take years for them to go through your product pipeline. For other industries, it's a quick process.

A Simple Example of a Product Sequence

In this example, I wanted to show you a simple product sequence. We only have a few layers that we go through and we do it on a horizontal plane. In just a little bit I'm going to show you a more detailed example with multiple layers and running vertically.

In this example we are looking at a company who sells a bag of potato chips. The initial starting point is giving out free samples at a grocery store.

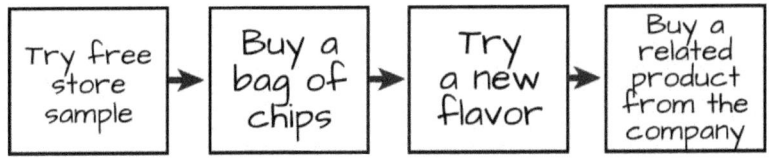

| Try free store sample | → | Buy a bag of chips | → | Try a new flavor | → | Buy a related product from the company |

Notice how the process continues. Similar to how our life evolves and we have different segments to our lives that continue, we have a purchasing segment that also moves forward in time with various products.

As you dig deeper into the purchasing sequence, one important point I want you to keep in the forefront of your mind is that if someone is buying your most expensive product or service there is room to make a more expensive product or service.

By now you are probably wondering what exactly a product pipeline is. A product pipeline is the sequence that a buyer goes through in their lifetime as they conduct business with you.

Industries such as the wedding industry have a small product pipeline and cycle. This means they don't get repeat customers frequently. The business is centered on word-of-mouth and referrals.

For example, if you are a wedding seamstress the bride comes and goes within a year. Your only bet for them to buy another dress from you is if they get divorced and remarried again (or have other dress alterations for you that are non-wedding related if you do those things).

How likely is that to happen? Even if they do get a divorce and get remarried how long will that take? 5 years? 10 years?

If you are in the car business, how long will that buying cycle take to repeat for your customer so that they come in and buy another car?

When people buy a brand new car most won't replace it within the next year or 3 years. These things take time to develop.

What you want to do is create a variety of products and services that a buyer can go through as they move through their life.

You will typically get the most sales in the lowest product tier.

This means the starting point of your cycle will typically sell the most amount of items.

Here is an example of my product pipeline in my stock education business on a simple level.

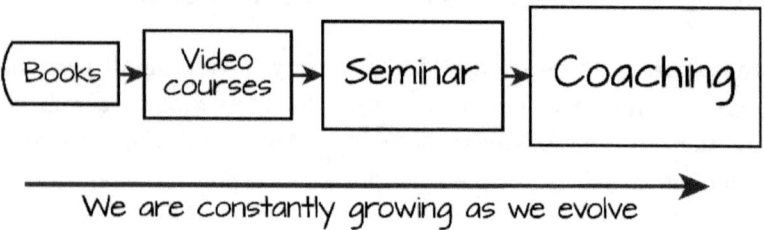

I call it the product pipeline because you are constantly moving people from a smaller product to a larger product just like from the sink in your home to your larger pipes under your home, the sewer, and finally the cleaning facilities. The process keeps growing with distance and the same should your products price or your customers' experience as they grow with you.

Here is an example of a lawn service company's product pipeline and the difference of a product pipeline that is growing and one that is at a standstill.

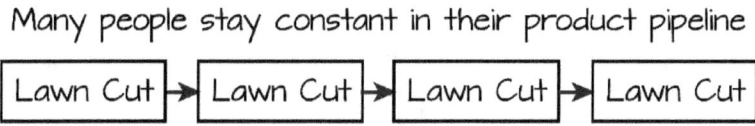

In the next diagram we apply value and price to the diagram to show you how it starts to affect your customers.

Your goal is to constantly grow and progress your products value which in return will give you more return

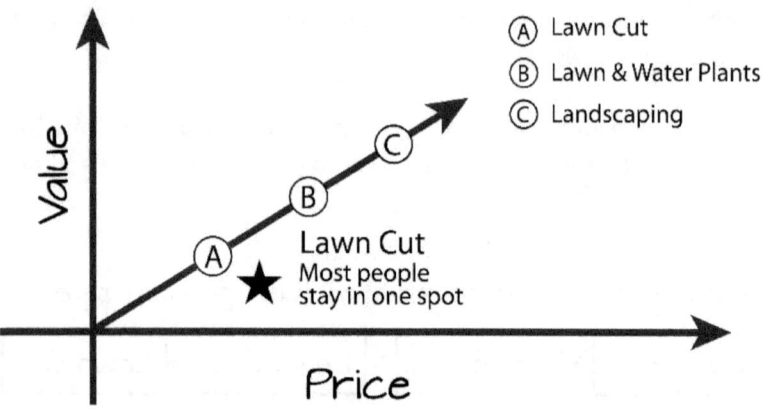

A Lawn Cut
B Lawn & Water Plants
C Landscaping

Lawn Cut
Most people stay in one spot

Rookie Mistake: Not having multiple product tiers for your customers to purchase and stopping at a certain level. Remember that if there are people buying your highest priced product you can always take them to a higher priced product.

I think by now you probably got a good grasp of the concept. I want to show you a more detailed example of my product pipeline rotated on a vertical plane. It may represent a funnel in this instance.

The way you look at the diagram whether it is a pipeline, a standard chart, or a funnel is not important. The end goal is all the same, which is to take your customers from a lower value to a higher value.

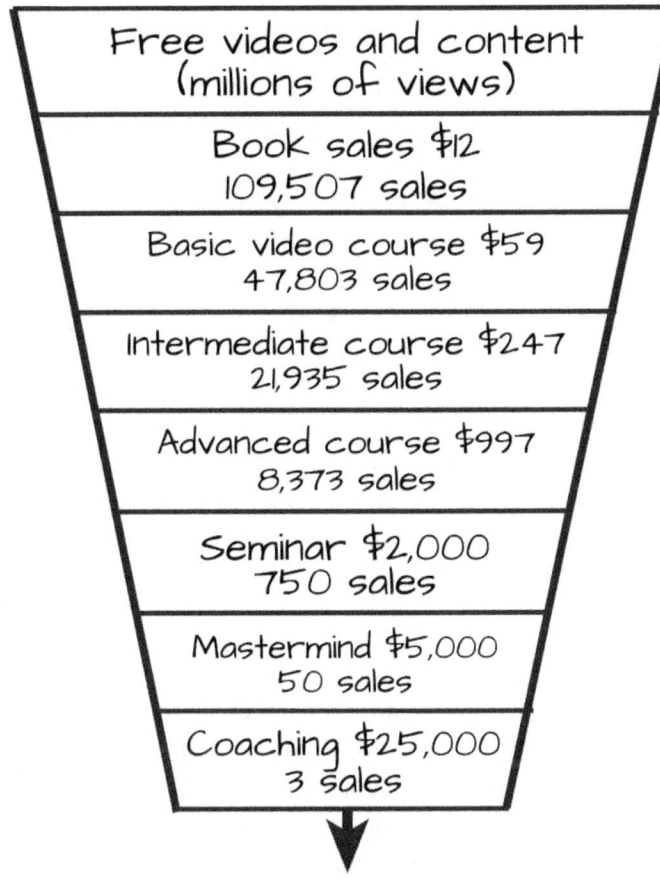

Free videos and content
(millions of views)

Book sales $12
109,507 sales

Basic video course $59
47,803 sales

Intermediate course $247
21,935 sales

Advanced course $997
8,373 sales

Seminar $2,000
750 sales

Mastermind $5,000
50 sales

Coaching $25,000
3 sales

If there are customers who are buying your highest priced product you can take them deeper to a higher price point

* Some sales and the price of products are hypothetical to give you an insight of how the process works *

In this example you can see that I'm going sell more video courses than seminars, and sell more books than video courses simply because it's a lower price item. The risks are less to the customer.

People who are new to investing are probably not going to want to attend a seminar or spend a lot of money. This is because at the beginning we don't want to risk a lot into something we are dabbling in whether that's risking our time, money, or energy.

This happens in nearly every industry simply because there are more beginners then there are experts.

Think of it as kids explore sports. They may at first try soccer. Then after a year or two they may play baseball, then jump to tennis, and the trend continues. Eventually we find a few hobbies that we stick with, but these things also change over the years based on our age, lifestyle, goals, and body. The same thing happens with products that we purchase and our interest.

For this reason you should always have multiple layers to your products from a free or low price point to a more expensive price point.

As people progress and get better they may build a deeper relationship with you and therefore purchase more expensive products. In my example, they may start with a small purchase such as a book and then if I added enough value they may choose to continue their education they may decide to purchase a small video educational course.

If they think that product was exceptional then the journey may continue.

Later, this could take them to an intermediate or advanced course, which could lead them to a seminar or private coaching.

I may only get a few private coaching students per year because not everyone is interested in that mastery level education.

The upside is they would be at a high price point such as $10,000 or $25,000, but it requires the most amount of my time since I spend a few hours per week with them.

The more personal something gets, the more expensive it gets because of the time and energy demands.

That's why a book is cheaper than a video course, and that's why coaching is more expensive than a video course.

We can dig further into this concept of products, how to properly set up the products, sequencing behind them, and much more in another book.

For now, the important thing to remember is that you want to move people from a lower price purchase or a free offer to a higher price purchase.

This process takes time for your customer to evolve whether that's their own personal knowledge and understanding of their problem or simply for them to be ready to purchase your product or service.

Make sure to have enough layers in your product pipeline where the jump between one segments to the next is not overly significant. For example you don't want to take people from a book purchase which is usually under $20 to a $1,000 product purchase as there can be many other steps in between that you are missing.

In industries such as roofing the price purchase is extremely high from the first purchase in part because it is a service along with material costs, but in addition remember that chances of you getting another roof within 5 years is highly unlikely.

The same goes with the wedding industry. It is a premium priced industry. You will pay premium dollars for a photographer, a dress, catering, even though if you wanted these things for any other regular night it would be cheaper and that is because in part the repeat business is not there and the costs for the company or service provider are high and future business potential from you (or their customer) is low.

So if you can build a product pipeline where your customers have multiple opportunities to connect with your product or service rather than a single instance you both win.

Chapter 9:
YOUR $100,000 YEAR WITH YOUR BUSINESS

In this chapter I wanted to share with you how you can actually get to $100,000 income stream per year with your blog business.

One of the reasons I choose a $100,000 is because of two reasons.

The first is that it is achievable because I've done it. The second is that many people strive for that six-figure income. Although one of the beauties behind hitting a six figure income is that studies have shown most people's happiness level beyond the $75,000 level is not any better than at $150,000.

The important point to learn from this chapter is that you are using your blog to solidify a foundation for you and for your business.

You take this foundation and then present products, services, and other various offers to your visitors and potential customers.

Keep in mind that it is the thing that you blog about, the things that you write about, and the information that you create video content around that will attract those types of people.

As you develop this content and center it around a primary focus, the customers that you attract will become more specific.

With highly targeted customers you have a higher probability of success when you present various product and service offers.

In order for you to become successful and reach a $100,000 income stream annually you need to know that it takes multiple products and service offers to get there. You typically won't do it by selling just one product nor will it happen within one transaction.

I hope by looking at these two different examples you get some ideas and insights of how a successful year can be broken down. It may take you a few years to get there, but if you build the right things you can see that it doesn't take 1 million sales to have some great results.

Product review blog

In this first example I wanted to show you a blog where a majority of the income is made through reviewing products and getting an affiliate commission for the sales.

Although not every product review blog will make the majority of its income from affiliate commission, I just wanted to share with you a concept that you can use and start thinking how this may or may not apply to you.

Blog category: Outdoor including camping, hunting, fishing, and boating.

Content examples:

- ★ Review of different crossbows and arrows
- ★ Reviews of top 5 or top 10 binoculars, riflescopes, night vision
- ★ Review of different lights, knives, tents, camp bedding, and camp furniture

At the beginning your content may target one specific niche such as only hunting or only fishing. As you expand and grow you can increase it to multiple areas under the big umbrella so think about your growth plan ahead of time.

It can then lead to camping, hunting, fishing, boating, and a few other sub-niches.

Income potential from affiliates:

Here is a breakdown of some numbers if you are aiming for a **$100,000** year with an affiliate commission review model along with a few other sources of income.

Category of Reviews	Sales / Week	Weekly Commission	Yearly Income
Fishing rods	10	$250	$13,000
Outdoor bedding	10	$250	$13,000
Tents	10	$250	$13,000
Hunting Knives	10	$250	$13,000
Survival Gear	10	$250	$13,000
Total	50	$1,250	$65,000

I have kept the commission percentage the same throughout all the product categories and items sold to keep the math simple. However note that this is not usually the case. Certainly, the larger the dollar value of the product that you sell the more commission you will earn.

For this example, in the chart above we are doing reviews in five different categories. It may take a few hundred videos of reviews to get to this point, but notice you only need about 10 sales per week per category to make up more than 50% of your $100,000 year.

You can supplement this income to get to your $100,000 year by creating a few informational products if you like and some sponsorship opportunities.

Income from sponsorship:

Often times if you have a popular blog or YouTube channel companies or people will pay you to promote a product or use a product during a video. They may even pay you to do reviews.

For this reason you may have heard in some videos phrases such as "this review or video is sponsored by... "

These video creators and reviewers are being paid to say that phrase. Not only will they receive commission from the sale of each item, but they may be getting paid to say a certain phrase, message, or even to wear some of the apparel that they do or use the phones that they use.

Let's break down the sponsorship income just a little bit.

Sponsor	Term Duration	Payment
Sponsor #1	One month	$2,000
Sponsor #2	Two weeks	$500
Sponsor #3	Three months	$5,000

Sponsor #4	Three months	$5,000
Sponsor #5	Four months	$6,000
Sponsor #6	Two weeks	$500
Total		$19,000

This means between your commission income and sponsorship income this puts you at $84,000 ($19,000 for sponsorship and $65,000 for affiliate income).

Income through your own products:

The final part is supplementing our income is through educational material (or your own products). I will use educational products in this example as we are focusing on a blog based business which is primarily information, but your products can be anything that you create or develop.

The beauty behind informational products is you earn nearly a 90% pure profit on the merchandise. It costs about $2.00 to manufacture a DVD or a book where you can sell a book for $10 or a DVD for about $50 or more depending on the material!

Let's say you had just 5 different book and/or DVD products and sold just a few of each per week. Here is the breakdown:

Product	Profit	Sold Per Week	Yearly Profit
Book #1	$7	5	$1,820
Book #2	$8	5	$2,080

DVD #1	$29	4	$6,032
DVD #2	$39	3	$6,084
DVD #3	$49	2	$5,096
Total			$21,112

In the above example I am assuming that you would sell more of the cheaper products (books) and less of the video courses as they are more expensive. Then even less of the most expensive video course.

Combining all income sources:

If we combine income from all three areas such as affiliates, sponsorships, and informational products here is what we get:

Income source	Yearly Total
Affiliate income	$65,000
Sponsorship income	$19,000
Educational products	$21,112
Yearly Income Total	$105,112

As you can see in this example that your income doesn't come exactly from one specific source. Meaning that it is not just one sponsor or one product that we sell. We have a distribution of income just in case we have any issues with our products, or favoritism between our customers, and so forth.

> **Rookie Mistake**: Trying to make all your income and money from one income stream. This can be dangerous if an issues arise. Diversification can bring stability and reduce risk.

I gave you this detailed example to show you that you only need to sell a few products a week within a few different categories to become quite successful.

In reality it may take you at least a year to get to this point and maybe two or three years because things take time to build. Nevertheless, I wanted to show you that you don't need big numbers to make a healthy living.

Growing your business further:

Once you have this content area of your business dominated, your next plan could be to become a wholesaler and distributor of these items much like what Amazon does with books and many other items.

Amazon does not personally create and manufacture every single item, however they have a trusting website where people purchase certain products. If you can do the same thing for a specific niche or category then rather pushing people to your affiliate's website, people would purchase products off of your website.

Here are some examples of niche related websites who distribute products in a few various niches.

- ★ http://www.cabelas.com/
- ★ http://www.gandermountain.com/
- ★ http://www.tennis-warehouse.com/
- ★ http://www.worldsoccershop.com/

★ http://www.tackledirect.com/

If you are looking to set this up in WordPress after doing reviews you simply need the Woocommerce plugin and a bit of customization.

Service business example

I wanted to share with you another example of how a $100,000 year can be created, but this time from a service business perspective focusing on still the blog business as a lead to bring people into your service business as well as selling educational products online.

In this example we will be focusing on a yoga business.

Yoga business: primary income from services, classes, seminars, and informational products.

Service based income:

Since the majority of our income will be focused on classes and services provided, we will be using the blog as a way to attract our customers.

You can apply this concept to many different businesses in providing a service to the end-user. This could be consultation services that you do online or something that you do more in person.

Class	Students	Monthly Income	Yearly Income
Mon + Wed	40	$2,800	$33,600

Tues + Thurs	40	$2,800	$33,600
Total	80	$5,600	$67,200

★ Income is calculated based on membership rates of $70/ month.

Educational products income:

Product	Profit	Sold Per Week	Yearly Profit
Book #1	$7	8	$1,820
Book #2	$9	7	$3,276
Book #3	$14	5	$2,080
DVD #1	$29	4	$6,032
DVD #2	$39	3	$6,084
DVD #3	$49	2	$5,096
Mastery Course	$97	1	$5,044
Total			$29,432

In this example I wanted to focus on splitting the revenue between informational products and your classes a bit more evenly just to show you if you decide to focus more on informational products that things are still achievable.

Even in this example we have multiple revenue streams. We have a service-based business where the blog is the primary driver to get people into the door. We also sell informational products online.

If you decide to focus more on one or the other, then of course you would have one products or classes to fit a certain income stream. This means if I wanted to only focus on online educational products then I would probably have many more books, video courses, and material.

Income from seminars or retreats:

Another possibility for income is to receive compensation for attending and speaking at seminars (or teaching) or even having your own seminar.

Teaching at a seminar	Pay
Seminar 1 (March)	$1,000
Seminar 2 (July)	$1,000
Seminar 3 (October)	$1,000
Total for the year	$3,000

Hosting your own 3-day seminar	Avg Price	Total
Attendees (200 people came)	$195	$39,000
Sell merchandise (50)	$25	$1,250
Total for the seminar		$40,250

★ Of course hosting your own seminar requires many elements and you may have a good amount of expenses. This means out of the $40,000 collected you may only make $20,000 in profit or even $12,000 depending on your expenses. Nevertheless still a fairly decent profit and a good credibility builder.

Combining all income sources:

If we take all these components and have them together the end result is quite good.

Income source	Yearly Total
Service income from students	$67,200
Educational products income	$29,432
Teaching at a seminar	$3,000
Hosting your own seminar	$40,250
Yearly Income Total	$139,882

In this chapter you got a chance to see multiple ways to create $100,000 income within different types of blog businesses.

Remember that you are using the blog business as your core. Then your income is created through multiple streams such as educational products, services you provide, affiliate products, or other methods.

Typically, it is not wise to have all of your income coming in from one thing or one source. Even the big movie stars don't make all of their income from any one single movie – it takes multiple streams of income to build wealth and the same is true for building a solid blog based business.

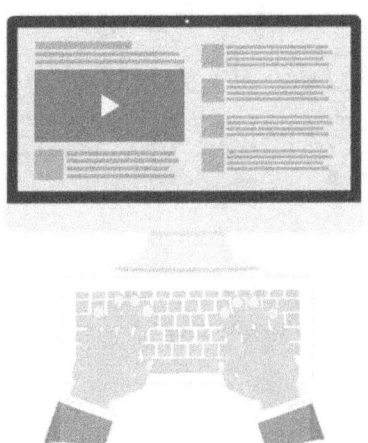

SECTION #2
PLANNING YOUR BLOG
BUSINESS & SETTING IT UP

CHAPTER 10:
HOW TO FIND A PROFITABLE NICHE THAT PAYS

Before you start building your blog business you need to claim a topic.

A niche is a specific topic that you're going to blog about, create products around, and dominate. If you blogged about everything in the world then that is not specific enough. People will not take you seriously or think of you as the expert.

Think about this: If you wanted a doctor, but the doctor you went to see had a part-time job as a body guard in the evenings and on the weekends he was a car mechanic. Then how much confidence would you have in him to be your doctor or to operate on you?

Probably very little. We look for expertise in someone and this helps build trust.

That means before you choose a niche you have to know that you can stick with that category for the long-term. If it's a category that you are not passionate about, then you probably won't have determination or discipline to stick to the topic for an extended period of time.

Empty market space

As we get into niches, I want you to know that a niche is not something that you come up with in your mind. A niche is something that is discovered.

It is an empty space in the marketplace that is focused on a specific audience where their needs are not being met or fulfilled to the maximum potential.

Take a look at this product quadrant that I created regarding shoe brands. I put the things that customers value on different ends of the spectrum (on opposite ends).

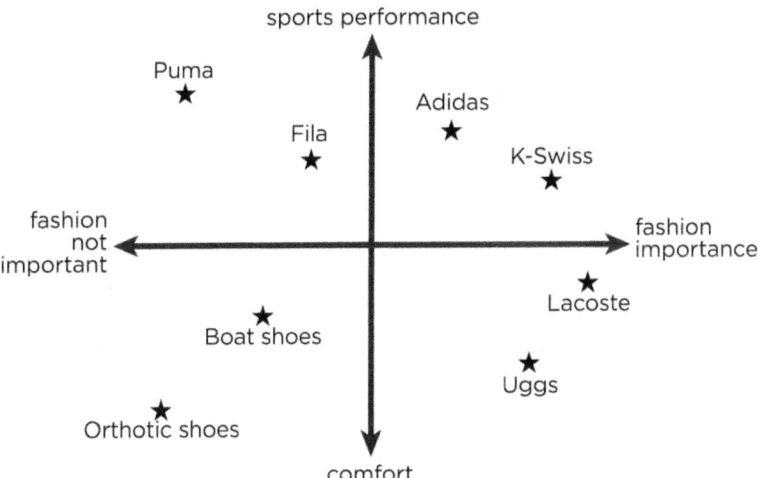

Position of the brands and shoe types are estimates and may not be accurate. They are there strictly for illustration purposes

In this example I used sports performance and comfort and related it to also the importance of fashion. I could have easily switched any one of these with high price and low price if I felt that was important to my customers or if that is what my research told me.

I could have even went with a different spectrum such as ecofriendly and non-environmentally friendly if this was important to my customers.

If I went with the eco-friendly route, I would be competing with shoe companies such as TOMS or other shoe companies who have global initiatives.

Nevertheless, you can see that certain brands are bit better for certain types of people. Other brands fit a different type of person.

Now this doesn't mean that people who prefer Adidas won't purchase boat shoes or Lacoste, but that simply means that their core ultimate preference during many purchasing moments will sway them to their default choice as this is their primary need (more athletic and somewhat fashionable).

The importance of this diagram is not exactly where things are positioned, but to find an empty space in the marketplace that can be fulfilled or improved.

This could be something that you blog about that makes their life easier, saves people money, or inspires them, people you may even save people time by providing great resources.

Finding a niche

One of the best ways to discover this empty market space is to personally talk to your potential customers.

If you have no idea of the primary category you're interested to get into then you could start with general questions such as:

★ What are the things that frustrate you? This will give you insight to their problems.

★ What things are you struggling with? This question will give you insight about what's difficult for them.

★ What have you tried in the past that has worked or that has not worked? This tells you about potential competitors or what is already available in the marketplace.

★ How could things be improved? This will give you insight to what they believe is the solution. This may save you time on research or give you ideas on marketing.

Unfortunately, starting with vague questions may lead you down the rabbit hole because not everybody thinks about these things off-the-cuff.

Not to mention, sensitive topics such as weight loss are not topics that most people will be inclined to open up about. This is why in certain instances it is better to observe people rather than to ask them direct questions.

If you already have a primary category in mind such as "fishing" you could ask questions such as:

What are some things that frustrate you when you are fishing? The answers may be something along the lines of:

★ I'm not catching any fish
★ I don't know what bait to use
★ I don't have a strategy for fishing tournaments

Once you get an idea of these different categories you might notice you have **recreational fishermen** and **competitive fishermen**. These are sub niches.

At this point you should get into the mind of your target customer. If they focus on recreational fishing then the questions you ask would be different than for a person who focuses on competitive fishing.

Think of it this way as well: who would probably purchase more products or spend more money on fishing gear? The recreational person or the competitive person?

More than likely the person who fishes competitively would spend more money on gear.

As you dig deeper about their past frustrations with the products or services that they tried, then you may get a better idea of what you could create or develop, and then see what's working and what's not.

At the beginning stage you may want to start with something simple such as selling other people's products. In this case, you would be an affiliate earning a commission on a per sale basis.

So how would you approach this concept?

Remember that near the beginning stages you have to add value to your customers and visitors. To do this, you may create different product reviews on fishing gear or equipment. You may even interview fishing experts which could create a great source of educational material.

Having two great areas like product reviews and expert interviews would attract the educational enthusiasts as well as the gadget people.

Towards the bottom of your review or on another page you may promote an offer these products which would earn you a commission after someone purchases.

As your blog business evolves, eventually you may decide to create your own product or offer a service. For example, you may design a new type of boat seat cover that stays cool during the scorching hot days or a place for people to stow their anchor when not in use (such as www.anchorstow.com).

Having your own physical products will give you flexibility and diversification in your product assortment. Often times having your own product will also give you the best margins when you make a sale.

If you decide to move with the digital route you could create "how-to" guides and training videos that of course you could sell.

Going deeper into specific topics is where you want to eventually get to such as:

★ How to prepare for your first fishing tournament!
★ How to win most fishing tournaments that you attend!
★ How to catch the biggest fish in the ocean!
★ How to catch more fish in less time and have more fun doing it!
★ The primary gear that you must have to catch more fish and how to use it!
★ How to choose your first fishing boat and not get ripped off!

The opportunities are endless!

Here is a quick example of our sequence of events to discovering our niche up until we create physical products.

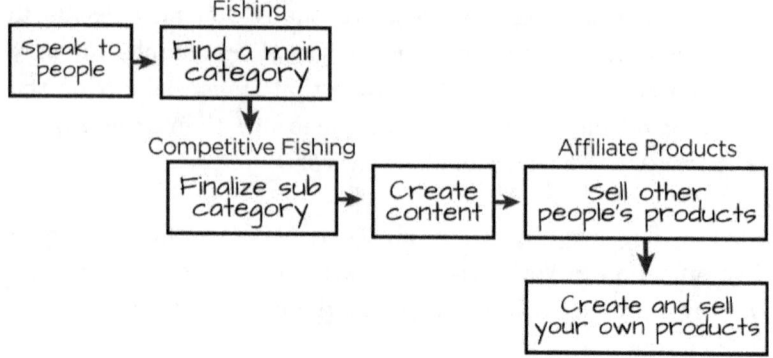

Defining your market audience

Keep in mind you are focusing your primary niche around a central topic or belief which is fishing, but you could get more specific and focus on recreational fishing or sports fishing and fine-tune things.

This way when people shop for products off your blog they feel as if it is made for them. This in turn often times creates a higher conversion of sales.

In marketing there are two primary ways to split people into categories.

1. **Demographics** such as a person age, race, location, or income.
2. **Psychographics** such as their core ideas, passion and beliefs.

When it comes to a blog business focusing your niche around demographics may limit your audience.

These days the Internet has made the world more connected and global. In essence you want to focus your niche around psychographics or in simple terms around a specific belief.

This could be a belief such as:

★ You should be able to cook and eat high quality organic food with ease. This may allow you to create a food blog and products focusing on great tasty organic recipes.

For example, if I focus only on age, most young adults between 10 and 20 years of age will not care about organic food. However, focusing on the core belief you may get a segment of people in that age group that care deeply about eating healthy.

Here is another example:

★ A woman should be able to defend herself if her life is in danger – this would allow you to create a blog about self-defense for women. You could sell products like flash lights, pepper spray, and other defensive products. You may even sell educational safety videos and books.

In this example, we eliminate the men and focus on the women. Products may be tailored to women such as smaller items since they typically have smaller hands.

As your audience grows and develops, in the future you can categorize them based on age, race, income, or any other demographics.

However until things are moving forward with your blog you want to stick to a central topic and core belief.

CHAPTER 11:
WHAT IS THE VALUE OF YOUR NICHE

As we continue to fine tune our niche, there is one last final point I want to make: **know the value of your niche.**

Financially poor niches

Besides being able to stick to a topic for an extended period of time, you need to ensure that your niche is a topic that has good capital or money flowing through it.

What I mean by this is that certain bloggers focus their efforts around topics where the target audience has no financial means to purchase products or they are against purchasing items all together.

If the audience that you are blogging to does not have the capability to purchase products, then you are betting on a dead horse – they have no money to buy your stuff!

From experience, most interests out there have money flowing through them. The hard part is properly positioning your niche, topic, or core message.

For example, a blog that is focused around coupon clipping will probably not have a wealthy audience. The belief around most people who clip coupons will be to save money.

In this case if you have a product such as a $75 coupon organizing notebook, then chances are the visitors that read your blog will not be interested in purchasing a product like that.

This may be because of their financial means or their beliefs are not in alignment with what you are offering. Nevertheless, you need to have a product that matches your customer based on the value of your niche. If you have a niche that has sustainable value than it makes things easier.

Now granted coupon clipping sites can be fantastic in terms of ad revenue because they attract a wealth of people and if traffic is high then it may produce healthy ad revenue.

Personally though, I would rather prioritize my income based on selling high-value products to a group of 100 customers for months or years in the future rather than worrying about search engines, advertising, and promotion for the rest of my life.

Everyone is different of course and what you choose is up to you.

The wealth of a niche

On the opposite side of the spectrum industries such as boat owners, airplane owners, real estate developers, medical doctors, or lawyers have more wealth around them.

This means if you target a niche around how to maintain your private airplane, where to park it when it's not in use, or equipment that you can purchase for your airplane then the content you create will attract people that are interested in those things. In other words the wealthy or people that can afford to do those activities.

In addition, if you have a product or service that you offer them in the future they will have the financial means to purchase it.

The knowledge of your niche's value is good to know. Check how valuable your niche is before jumping in. One of the ways you can do this is by looking at keyword bids on Google Ad Words.

This method won't give you exactly how valuable a niche is, but it will give you an idea of which niches have more money flowing through them. If it is expensive to bid on a keyword then most likely that industry has money flowing through it (and of course has competition).

On the other hand there are niches that are undiscovered, have no keyword bidders, and people are not asking for the product or service, but they are screaming inside of them to have it!

Regulated niches

Finally, watch out for niches with high regulations. Personally, I wouldn't want to be in a blog industry that has many regulations.

This may include niches like smoking, guns, adult industry, or medical drugs.

Although some of these can be lucrative, there are many bureaucratic regulations that you will need to account for once you start selling products in these categories.

Final words on niche value

In the end, strive to find a niche that has money flowing through it. It doesn't have to be the wealthiest niche in the world, but you don't want to sell to kids who have five dollars in their pocket. The only way to make that work is by large traffic quantities in sponsorships since they don't have the means to buy.

In addition, you should watch out for regulated niches unless you know what you are doing in that industry with 100% certainty because there could be a lot of headaches and stressful pitfalls with them.

CHAPTER 12:
CREATING A BLOG NAME THAT IS UNFORGETTABLE

Once you've picked out your category and niche, you might be ready to create your blog name.

Before I build or create anything new whether that's writing, creating a new blog, creating a product, or even writing a new book I always think carefully and meticulously about the name.

Choosing a name can be difficult.

Many people often times choose a name to reflect ourselves and we want it to represent us. That is a huge mistake!

In the past, I made the mistake about creating business names that have to do with me or used my name. It used to be a personal vendetta to get my name out there.

However, remember that when you're dealing in business it's not about you – it's about your customer. That is what you should focus on when you are creating a blog name.

Your blog is about your audience. It is about your customer.

You need to have a name that matches them and that name that they can connect to and relate to. It's not about you having a blog that is named after you (unless you are a famous celebrity).

In essence, you want to create a name for your blog that is unforgettable!

Many people may say that you should make it easy to remember, but if you could make it unforgettable then you are one step ahead.

I understand that it is not easy to make things unforgettable, but if you strive for that goal then at least you might create a killer name that's easy to remember.

For those of you who are more analytical and want a systematic approach to creating a blog name, or any name for that matter, I will share with you a few ways that I approach naming.

By going with a systematic approach I think it makes things easier especially as you start developing products, naming your services, or anything else that comes your way.

Here are four systematic ways you can use to name anything:

* ★ **Alliteration:** which means having the same sound at the beginning of two words. This does not necessarily mean the same letter although that does help.
* ★ **Rhyme:** repetition of similar sounds
* ★ **Rhythm:** strong repeat of sounds
* ★ **Power Association:** strong influence

One important point that I want to emphasize before you start naming your blog is that people remember things based on the way they sound – not the way they are spelled.

If you are creating a blog name on your own, say it out loud and listen to the sounds.

In this situation you will get a 1st person perspective sound which sounds differently than a 3rd person perspective. Similar to how your voice on an answering machine or your voice on video sounds different than when you speak to someone.

To go to a deeper level you can record yourself on video or a voice recorder saying different names out loud and play them back to yourself. You should get a slightly different variation.

Lastly, I know that sometimes names can have sexy or curvy letters that look great on paper, but once the name is created, focus on how it sounds because you will need it to flow off the tongue rather than having nice letters that you can use to make an awesome logo with.

Here are some examples of different blogs with some creative names:

Alliteration:

★ Sunday Suppers http://www.sunday-suppers.com/
★ Seven Spoons http://sevenspoons.net/
★ Glamour and Grace http://glamourandgraceblog.com/
★ Travel-Tot http://travel-tot.com/

Rhyme:

★ PopPhoto http://www.popphoto.com/
★ Rock the Shot http://www.rocktheshotforum.com/
★ Cocktails & Details http://cocktailsdetails.com/blog

Rhythm:

★ The Delicious Life - http://www.thedeliciouslife.com/
★ Teeny Tiny Kitchen http://www.teenytinykitchen.com/
★ Cambridge in Colour
   http://www.cambridgeincolour.com/

Power Association:

* ★ Stone Soup - http://thestonesoup.com/blog/
* ★ The Auto Prophet http://theautoprophet.blogspot.com/
* ★ Breaking Muscle http://breakingmuscle.com/
* ★ Ultra Runner Girl http://ultrarunnergirl.com/

Some blog names use a combination of these techniques such as

* ★ Girls Gone Strong http://www.girlsgonestrong.com/. You could say this name uses power association and alliteration.
* ★ Backpack to Buggy http://www.backpacktobuggy.com/ again could be a rhythm and alliteration

The thing that matters is not which technique to use. It is a way to get you to think about some ideas so that you can create a powerful name that is unforgettable for your blog business!

CHAPTER: 13:
SETTING UP YOUR BLOG

Once you have your name and a preliminary plan for your product pipeline then you are ready to set up the infrastructure for your blog and make it live online.

Setting up your blog is not that difficult even if you want to do the work yourself. It will require about half an hour of your time if you're completely brand-new but somewhat computer savvy.

If you don't know much about computers, it may take you half a day or you may want to hire someone to set it up for you. You could of course pay someone on Fiverr.com to help you as well which may just cost you less than $20 to get a basic WordPress website setup and installed.

The steps I will outline won't give you a fancy template, but it will get you up and running. You can always change the color and appearance later.

Choosing a platform

There are a few different blogging platforms available that you can choose from.

The platform is how your blog is going to be running. Think of it like the engine that runs the truck or the sedan. Every engine will have advantages and disadvantages similar to how a big truck can tow a big load, but an electric coupe gets better gas mileage.

1. **WordPress.org** is my personal favorite because it allows you to grow the blog into a business and continue to expand as your business grows. The flexibility of the platform is fantastic and support online is easy to find.

Note: There are two versions of WordPress. WordPress.com and WordPress.org. WordPress.com allows you to get a free WordPress site such as http://www.yourname.wordpress.com. This is horrible if you decide to go with your own dot.com in the future as all your marketing efforts would be wasted!

Wordpress.org is where you download the WordPress core files (absolutely free) and then upload these files to your website host. This is the version that you want.

This is what would allow you to have your own dot com (meaning your website would be self-hosted).

As your blog business grows you definitely will need to self-host your website.

WordPress.org is my recommendation (not WordPress.com). WordPress.com would be fine for a personal blog.

2. **Blogger.com** is another option to set up a blog. Unfortunately your name includes a .blogspot. As example it would be "yourname.blogspot.com." Again, for this reason I would avoid Blogger.com.

3. **Tumblr.com** – you may have heard Tumblr as it is quite easy and an extremely popular blogging platform. Sadly, there are many limitations.

If you are serious about your blog business you need a blogging platform that will allow you to set things up based on your needs and allows you to grow.

I mentioned these other platforms so you don't get sucked into setting up your blog the wrong way.

As technology evolves, if you happen to find another platform that works that has flexibility, has a dot com that you own, and allows you to expand with shopping carts or payment systems then there is nothing wrong with going that platform.

However as of today, WordPress.org is one of the best choices in my opinion.

Step #2: Domain Name

Once you decide the blogging platform, you will need to setup a few more things which would include your domain name, website hosting, and install your WordPress files (and customize your website).

Domain name is your dot com on the internet. This can be a .net, .org, or one of the many extensions are available.

Personally I would go with a dot.com because this is what most people default to when they think of a website address.

A domain can be purchased for around $10 per year. If you want to add some level of privacy so people can't back check your domain registration details it could be as much as $20 per year (or of course you could just get a P.O. Box). Different registers charge different amounts.

I personally use Godaddy.com to register my domains.

When choosing a domain, your first choice might be taken. Don't stress it!

★ Try to avoid hyphens in your domain name.

★ Watch out for beginnings and endings that start with the same letter when joining words as unintentional connotations could be troublesome.

Here are some examples of troubling domains

★ Cameraapparel.com (notice the two A's some people may go with camerapparel.com)

★ Expertsexchange.com ("experts exchange" or is it "expert sex change")

★ Speedofart.com ("speed of art" vs "speedo fart")

I wanted you to see these domain name issues ahead of time so you don't make the same mistake. People will see different things as they read so think of all the variations carefully as you choose your domain.

Step #3: Web Hosting

A web host is the server that your website sits on.

Think of this as a computer that is on 24 hours a day so people can access your website at any time. Normally you can purchase website hosting for as little as $5 per month.

The more traffic your website receives, along with the more content you post the more you'll need to have a powerful server. In this case, you may be paying $20, $100, or $1,000 per month depending on the popularity of your blog.

The website hosting requirements will depend on two factors:

★ The disk space you are using

★ The bandwidth or traffic coming to your website

If you want to see who I use for hosting or anything else visit my list of resources at: http://www.backstageincome.com/resources/

To save yourself some time, in many instances you can purchase your website hosting with your domain name. This usually simplifies things for most people. If you go to your website hosting company they may have an option for you to register a domain name at the same time you purchase hosting.

Tip: Sometimes your hosting company will give you a free domain name if you purchase hosting for one year in advance.

Prepaying your hosting for a year in advance helps offset the costs of paying your registration fees, which even the web hosting company has to pay.

In addition, many times your website host can install WordPress for you automatically with a push the button.

This means you would not have to download any files, and would make your life a little bit easier.

CHAPTER 14:
DESIGNING YOUR BLOG

Once you have your blog installed, you may need to set up a few things to have it looking professional and running correctly. Many of the things in your blogging platform will be fairly intuitive.

The navigation menus are fairly easy to understand for the most part and if you spend about 30 minutes with a basic WordPress overview video you will learn quite a bit on how to use the platform.

Tip: If you want to watch the video course that accompanies this book, then visit http://www.rise2learn.com where I go in detail about how to install WordPress and a basic overview of WordPress.

Remember that the thing that you should focus on when setting up your blog is not the design. It is more important to focus on the right functions, the content, and adding value to your visitors rather than how fancy or pretty your website looks.

The goal of your website and what you want people to think when they visit your blog is that "I learned so much," or "it was fantastic and I got a lot of knowledge out of that," or "that made me laugh so hard!"

Instead, many designers or blog owners want people to say "wow I really love the colors or the design of your website. It looks so beautiful."

The thing is, no one is going to give you money because the design of your blog looks great or because you picked nice colors. After all, how many times did you make purchase online because you loved the website's color scheme?

The design helps make browsing and purchasing slightly easier, but it is not the number one priority of a website no matter how much a designer tells you it is.

There are a few key important things that you do want to set up within your blog.

* **Permalinks** which will make your blog posts friendly to search engines such as **http://www.yourname.com/blog-post-name/** rather than **http://www.yourname.com/?p=25193**
* **Yoast Seo plugin** will allow you to add a title and description tag for the search engines for each new post that you write.
* **Ithemes security** (or some security plugin) which will help prevent hackers (or at least make things a bit harder for them).
* **Backup Wordpress** – which is a good plug-in to backup all your data from your blog. After all, it is a business so you want to back up your files once a week or at least once a month depending on the popularity of your blog.

You never know when you will need to restore files and hard drives if you have a computer crash, so always have a plan to back up!

* **Woocommerce** (or an ecommerce plugin) - if you plan to sell products (which I would assume you would be since this is a business) something like Woocommerce would be a good plugin to install

★ **S2member or Wishlist** – if you plan to have a membership program or a continuity program for content then S2member and Wishlist are the top choices currently in the membership.

One last final thing you may want to install is a custom theme.

WordPress has many free or low-cost themes available that you can download!

By installing a free theme, this of course would make your website possibly similar to 100 or 5000 other websites out there. However, looking at the bigger picture among millions of blogs, does it matter that much to you to have a unique identity at the beginning of your journey?

In fact, many of those other websites are probably not in the same niche as you or they may have customized the theme.

I think many people focus heavily on their design at the beginning due to their ego or they want to show their individuality. We want uniqueness and brand recognition. However, when you first start out you have no brand, nor will you get any recognition until you start giving value to others.

You need your design to be clean and easy to browse, but you don't need to waste time on a fancy color scheme or an amazing logo at the beginning stages. You can add these things in a few months when you have the initial aspects complete and have a foundation built.

If your content is interesting or engaging then that is what people are looking for. If something is interesting, then we will read it for hours. If it's not interesting then we move on.

I can't stress this enough!

Focus on adding value to your customers with your content and information. After three to six months you can develop a nice design that you like and your visitors may enjoy.

Remember that at the beginning focus on the core fundamentals. Get the basic things set up in WordPress such as a backup plugin, something to help with the search engines, tweak your permalinks so they are friendly, make sure the security is up to date, and then get a basic theme to get you started.

Once you have a good foundation and your blog is receiving steady traffic, you are consistent at posting, and you are starting to gain traction, then by all means feel free to go out and tweak those things that are of less importance.

CHAPTER: 15:
HIRING SOMEONE TO DO WORK

As you continue to work on your blog and you complete the right actions to grow it, you will reach a certain point where you need a helping hand with the workload.

I always say, if I can hire someone to do the work, even if it's 70% as good as I would do it, then I win.

The reason is 70% results with 0% of my effort or time is better than 100% results with 100% of my time and effort.

I value my time and energy because you can always make more money, but you can't buy more time.

There will be a certain point where you may want a custom theme for your blog, maybe help in writing content, help managing your social media profiles, or someone to help you with answering your emails. At that point, it would be time to hire someone to help you with the administrative tasks.

You, as the blog business owner, should be focusing on four primary things. Those things include:

1. Connecting with your customers or visitors
2. Marketing your blog business and your products
3. Creating and developing new products, coming up with service expansion ideas, or adding value to your customers
4. Relaxing so that can balance out your mental processes

Administrative tasks like responding to email questions, cleaning floors, managing social media profiles, grammar and spelling checking, or video editing are administrative tasks that you can pass to someone else.

Virtual Assistant

A virtual assistant is typically the person that you want to hire to handle some of these things.

A virtual assistant is your go to person online that will take care of many of your online administrative tasks.

Many of them usually can't do specialized tasks like video editing and at the same time be great at proofing your e-books as everyone has their strengths.

Although they can help you with some tasks that will allow you to free up some of your time to focus on other things, whether that is creating additional products or just having a little bit more free time.

The beauty is if you could pay someone $5 to $10 per hour to help you take care of 5 hours of tasks, then you save 5 hours of your time per week where you could focus your time and energy on the more important things in your life.

This may not be realistic at the beginning when you are first getting started with the blog business, but as you become busy with managing customers, handling orders, or marketing then you would have some income coming in. This means if you can save a few hours each week!

Personal Assistant

You could look at saving time in another way such as getting rid of the administrative tasks you have to do at home.

If you wanted to do the online tasks yourself at the beginning, but you have many chores at home such as washing dishes, doing the laundry, cutting the grass, or cleaning, you could hire a personal assistant to take care of those tasks for you.

Again, if you could save 5 or 10 hours per week, it would allow you to spend your time on the more important things that would grow your business rather than washing dishes.

Most people know how to wash dishes and you can easily find someone to cut your grass. However, it is very difficult to find someone that has the exact the goals and knowledge to create a business for you that is specific to your needs. This is something only you can do.

Of course you don't want to hire a personal assistant until your blog is developed with great content, has a product or sales offer, and is starting to generate a few sales per month. This would reassure you that you are doing the right things, and not blowing your money at the beginning simply to use your business as an excuse to have an easier life.

I understand at times you may need help because you don't know how to do something, but to have a regular assistant you should at least have some consistency in your business.

When you are ready to hire someone to help you with the administrative tasks or you want a custom theme, then there are a few ways that you can approach this.

★ **Freelancing websites** such as odesk.com or freelancer.com are a great starting place to get a virtual assistant or a theme developer.

On these websites you post an online task or job requirement that you would like to complete and then people bid on your project. You can then select a person that matches your specifications, or peaks your interest such as the price you're willing to pay, their experience, or based on their portfolio.

★ **Local methods** – if you have a high school or college nearby then you could post something locally such as a flyer to see if any students are interested in some work on the side. This could be someone to design your website theme or someone to do your administrative work.

★ You can apply the same concept on Craigslist if you're looking for someone to take care of your administrative household chores or help you with online related tasks. Someone local may be great if you prefer someone nearby that you can talk to or show them exactly what to do. However take precautions as you would with anyone else and be clear on your expectations.

When hiring someone – start slow. Do not overwhelm them with a huge batch of complicated work at the beginning. Give them a medium-difficulty task to prove to you they can handle it before you give them more complicated or larger tasks.

If you give them a task that is too easy then maybe anyone can fulfill it and you won't see if they are truly qualified. If you give them a task that is too difficult it may overwhelm them and it won't allow your relationship to build.

Starting out this way will give you a chance to see if the relationship works and if they can handle your needs.

It's quite possible that they may be interested, have the skill set, and available to do your website theme which is something that you may do once every two years, but they may not be available each week to help you with the administrative tasks.

That is why I say start slow and develop a relationship with time. Usually it takes a couple of months to see if someone is going to work well for the long-term.

I can't tell you the number of people that I have hired where things were working great for the first month and later they stop working or just disappear.

There are many reasons of why this happens, but be prepared, as it does happen.

For this reason it is important for you to be clear on your expectations. I will typically rephrase things multiple times in my job posting to ensure that I am clear and so that I attract the right person and one who understands my expectations.

For example, if I am looking for an administrative assistant here is an example of a posting that I may do:

"I'm looking for an administrative assistant that can transcribe videos into articles.

If you are someone who is familiar with WordPress and have experience with writing articles then I might be interested in you! On the other hand if you struggle navigating your way online then this job may not be a great fit.

Normally I post 10 videos per month on topics related to business, Internet marketing, stock trading, and investing.

If you have experience in any of these niches, then you might be who I'm looking for. However, if you struggle with understanding words such as 'dividend' or 'sales funnel' then it's best if you do not apply.

Typically you will need to spend on average 5 to 10 hours per week to complete the tasks. You can work at any time of the day, but you should have excellent communication and a good vision for hitting deadlines.

I'm looking for a teammate for at least six months and someone to be my go-to person. If you're the type of person that is looking for quick cash for the next month then please do not apply.

On the other hand if you are looking for a long-term relationship with growth that will teach you about business and the online space then you might be perfect!

If you think you fit the profile above and believe you are a perfect match then I would love to hear from you!

Please apply below by letting me know what is it that you enjoy about working online."

Take a look at the detail that I went into on this job post – it's quite extensive. Probably more extensive than what you would find online for many job postings.

Compare this to:

"I need a virtual assistant to help me manage my cooking blog."

The reason I go in such great detail is to weed out the candidates that are not a great fit for me.

My time and energy is valuable and it takes a great deal of my resources to find someone, build a relationship, teach them what to do, and navigate the communication gaps. I want to minimize the hassle, time, and energy with this process as much as possible.

You can apply this same concept to hiring someone to design your website theme, or for a local personal assistant. Just be as detailed as possible such as including examples of websites that you like.

You will definitely need someone to eventually help you with your blog as things grow.

Start preparing yourself now and look for those super star players!

CHAPTER 16:
CONTENT HIERARCHY

Developing content for your blog is a large task that you will have as a blog owner.

With a blog website most of your value is added to your visitors in the form of content.

Before we get into the specifics of the content, think about the highest content form possible that you can give to your audience.

Here is a content hierarchy chart for you to get you to start thinking about content hierarchies to see what I'm talking about.

Content Hierarchy

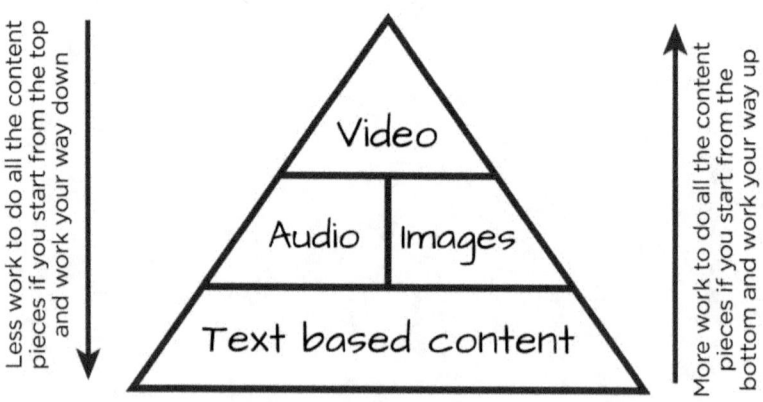

As you can see from the above diagram, videos are the highest content form at this time.

The reason I say that videos are the highest content form is because there is a lot of data within a video.

For example, I can extract the audio from a video and add that audio to a podcast. I can extract certain frames or images from that video and add those photos within my blog post. This could create a text blog or transcription people can read or download.

All the words that were said in the video could be transcribed by your virtual assistant and added into your blog post.

As you can see, from one video I can extract multiple content mediums.

That's powerful stuff!

As a little side note; search engine's put higher value on videos because they take more effort to create. It is for this reason why you often see thumbnails of videos next to your Google search results when searching for something online.

If you aren't strong at producing video content or the niche you are in is not video oriented, then stick to a content medium that fits with your audience.

You don't have to do everything. You just have to add value to your audience in the way they like to receive it.

However know the bigger picture and the value of different content mediums because if you are willing to push yourself and do a little bit of learning then you may be able to produce great video content within a short amount of time.

CHAPTER 17:
CONTENT TOPICS

The next stage is to start creating your content topics and ideas to blog about.

Normally, you want to focus on ideas that lead your prospect to the next stage in your purchase cycle. Think of this as going back to your product pipeline and guiding people through each step.

If you're going to be blogging about scuba diving, then you probably will want to lead to a product purchase of something such as a scuba diving book, certification, or hot zones classified dive report.

If you're blogging about dogs then you want to lead your audience to something related to dog training, breeding, health products, and something else related to dogs.

Remember that you constantly want to grow your prospect to the next product or sale that you are going to be offering.

This isn't only about you making money from them, but about evolving them as a person in their topic of interest (which is your niche).

Before you start posting content on your blog, you want to create a schedule that you can follow.

A schedule does two things for your business.

1. Allows you to stay consistent with your content and posts.

2. Allows your readers or viewers to expect content at a certain interval.

If you post your content sporadically then being disorganized is going to bring inconsistency to your business and nag at your emotions as you won't have a rhythm. It is similar to how a horse has a certain rhythm or pace. If you are not in that rhythm then you won't have a smooth ride.

The bigger issue will be with your audience. If you're posting sporadically such as one thing on August 5th, then August 20th, then September 12th how do they know when you're going to release new information?

How will you connect with them consistently? You won't be able to if you post inconsistently.

People love consistency. It is the reason why we typically eat the same breakfast meals day after day. It is the same reason why we hang out with the same type of people, whether that's our church friends, dance friends, sports friends, or business colleagues.

Think of the major TV shows and how they conduct their business. They have a predetermined time slot that they follow week after week even though the season has already been filmed. They could release everything on Monday and have 12 episodes of your favorite show, but they don't do that!

They release things periodically on a consistent basis so that viewers continue to tune in. This, in essence, brings them more advertising revenues throughout a longer timeframe and gives them consistency. For example, they can predict or estimate the number of viewers each week.

You can do the same thing with your blog if you build an audience that comes to read or watch your content on a consistent basis, but for this, you need to have a schedule.

Typically I would recommend posting something at least once every two weeks. This keeps you in the back of your audiences' minds. Posting any less than two weeks and your audience may forget about you.

Personally, I try to post once per week. In a full year, this would give me 52 posts, videos, or content pieces. That is not that many when you think about it.

In a single day, I can knock out and create about 10 blog posts on a Saturday. When I first started, it took time to figure things out and it may have taken me a whole day to create one content piece.

The reason it took me a whole day was because I hated the way I was presented on video, little nuances that I said, my hand gestures, and my voice. I just seemed more robotic. You can see the difference between my previous videos and my most recent ones. However, after making dozens of videos I spoke more naturally and relaxed in front of the camera which made my videos exceptionally better.

In your case it may take you a little bit longer to create content at the beginning, but as you get better you will become quicker and more efficient.

Start slowly with your content pieces and if things evolve with your blog you can increase the posting time frames. You can then start posting two or three times per week. One thing that you don't want to do is overwhelm yourself and then have to reduce your posting amount.

The better route is to start small and then later increase as you get into the flow. Never decrease the amount of content you are creating because this will hurt you in terms of leadership expectations, search engines (since they like content), and a few other ways.

Now create a posting schedule that you can follow consistently. I find that sticking to a weekday such as a Tuesday or Wednesday or any other day that you choose is the better approach.

Typically I try to avoid weekends just because many people are busy or doing other things than their normal habitual lives that they live Monday through Friday, but every audience will be different depending on the niche and you may have to experiment with when your target audience is online the most.

So what's going to be your posting schedule?

Here are a few examples of some posting schedules. Keep in mind you can increase the posting schedule all the way to multiple times per day, but this is only recommended for highly mature blogs and websites.

Light posting schedule (every 2 weeks)

Mon	Tues	Wed	Thurs	Fri	Sat /Sun
		Blog Post			

General posting schedule (every week)

Mon	Tues	Wed	Thurs	Fri	Sat /Sun
		Blog Post			
		Blog Post			

More aggressive posting schedule

Mon	Tues	Wed	Thurs	Fri	Sat /Sun
	Blog Post		Webinar or video		
	Blog Post		Webinar or video		

CHAPTER 18:
GENERATING CONTENT

There may be a time when you get stuck at a roadblock thinking about creating content and you will need to come up with fresh ideas.

All your ideas regarding your content should focus on your customer's frustrations, struggles, things that excite them, or anything that has a high emotional value.

One of the simplest ways to create new content ideas if you are stuck is to start by browsing topics or interests that other bloggers discuss in your industry. This may spark a few ideas. Of course, don't plagiarize, but take a look at some headlines and see if ideas spark up.

One important point is that you want to ensure that you're bringing something new to the table. You don't want to be posting the same content as someone else. Eventually it will get discovered. In simple terms, you don't want to regurgitate information. Distinguish yourself from the crowd.

The thing you should remember is that there is an unlimited amounts of content that can be created. Even though someone might have created a content piece about how to train your dog to sit, there may be a different way to explain it or present it.

For example to show how you can teach a dog to sit you could

1. Explain it by talking about the process (theory)
2. Show the process by you demonstrating it with a dog

3. Show the process with a dog that is not cooperating and how to make adjustments in your training
4. Show 3 variations of how to teach a dog to sit using different commands and ways
5. Show how to teach a dog to sit with a physical command or hand signals
6. Demonstrate how to teach a dog to sit using a noise or audio command or even a foreign language
7. Show the timeframe through time lapse videography or footage of how to train a dog to sit over the course of the week or a month

There are seven variations above to give you some ideas. The list goes on and the only limit is your creativity, teaching ability, or communication skills in getting your point across.

If you did the content with audio, video, or articles, that can give you three ways for each variation.

The truth is that certain concepts will relate better to certain people and other methods may be better for other people. Everyone prefers different learning styles, different types of entertainment, and different ways to connect to content.

If you present a variety of methods, techniques, or concepts to present the same material, you will be more to appealing to a larger audience.

Rephrasing concepts may feel the same to you, but as a visitor we are picky about the content that we connect with.

To summarize, get more specific in your content and strive to connect to your audience in various ways.

The possibilities are unlimited so start getting your creative juices going!

CHAPTER 19:
THE TOPICS OF DISCUSSION

Creating content will be time-consuming if you don't have a system in place. It's going to drain you! Not to mention it will be in the back of your mind as you work on other things if you are trying to stay consistent in your posting schedule.

One of the first things that I do before I create content is come up with categories for the blog posts. If I have the categories set up then you will know the topics you can dig deeper into.

The way I set up my categories is based on the products that I plan to have in the future. You may not be able to know every product that you plan to have, but I plan for the end goal as best as I can.

This means if I know I want to have a product on "writing and creating e-books" and one about "creating a money making podcast" then I would focus on having two categories in my blog such as "e-books" and "podcasting." then I would create blog content around these topics to attract people who are interested in these subjects.

If I wanted to sell products that are for camping enthusiasts such as camping knives, fire starters, or tents, my categories could be knives, tents, fire equipment. I may create blog content about reviewing different camping knives or fire starters. I may even create videos about how to set up your camping tent.

My goal and purpose is to post content on topics that my potential customer would be interested in. This helps attract the people I want, so that I can build trust, and later present an offer.

Have you heard of the power of attraction?

Everything that you say, talk about, and the energy you give off attracts a certain type of person. This applies to your blog business and it applies to your daily life. To prove it to you, take your five closest friends, average them together, and the end result is you.

If in your blog business, your goal is to attract customers for specific products that are interested in certain things then you need to be discussing and talking about those topics.

In the end your topics of discussion should be focused on your end customer. In the marketing world, we call this your avatar. Make each item as focused and targeted to this avatar as you can so that they can't wait to get more from you!

CHAPTER 20:
THE LIFESPAN OF YOUR CONTENT, PRODUCTS, & BUSINESS

When you take a look at the world around you, in the big scheme of things, we all have a certain amount of time on this planet. For some people it is 100 years or more. For other people it may be much less.

Everything has a certain shelf life, including your content, your products, and your blog business.

Typically, content shelf life is shorter than a products shelf life. Your products shelf life is typically shorter than a business shelf life. This is due to again the hierarchy pyramid.

If we take a look back at the digital camera revolution one of the things that Kodak struggled to do was create digital cameras. The shelf life of their past cameras (film cameras) became obsolete within a few years after digital cameras were released.

Their business suffered dramatically because they didn't catch on to the trend and didn't think about the shelf life of their product.

Their business could have gone down the drain, but fortunately they were able to survive and finally catch up in order to survive.

Companies that don't continue to innovate or keep up with evolution eventually die such as many railroad companies in the 1900's that died when the automobile become more affordable and mainstream.

Even today, think about Blockbuster or Yahoo – although not fully dead yet, they are struggling for market share and are being replaced by other companies such as Netflix and Google.

With a blog business, you too have a shelf life. It more pertains to your content and products, but you still have to think about it and make adjustments if necessary.

Before you start creating a blog or creating content, think about the type of content that you are creating.

When we zoom our focus into the weekly or general content that you will be creating there is time sensitive content such as news, and content that is evergreen that you can post at any time.

When I first started my stock trading blog I could have taken it in two different directions:

- ★ **Path #1:** Each week I could talk about the hot stocks for the week.
- ★ **Path #2:** Give tips regarding overall strategies, techniques, and insights.

I took the second option because if I created videos regarding current hot stocks, those videos would be useful for people that were watching my videos that week! After that, my content would be less relevant, maybe even useless or worse – dead!

If I took the first approach I could have fresh content each week with news, but it would make it difficult to keep up with.

Since I took the second route and included tips, strategies, techniques, and insights rather than the current daily stock market news it allowed those videos to be timeless.

They won't stand the test of time forever (at least I don't expect them to), but it is more likely that they could get a good five years of viewership. Meaning people would watch it five years from the day I publish the content and it could still be beneficial.

Every industry, niche, product, or blog has as a certain lifespan and it is important to know your lifespans in your business whether it's your products, content, or industry.

Lifespan of your content
───▶

Lifespan of your products
───▶

Lifespan of your business
───▶

If you create a blog based on technical support for seniors who do not know how to use a computer and your plan is to have products such as learning Microsoft Word 2013, then this category has a certain lifespan.

Software with time gets updated and new versions get released. In our Microsoft Word example, every few years there is usually an updated version.

This means you have anywhere between 2 to 3 years to capitalize on your information if you started making posts at the beginning of the software launch.

This doesn't mean that people will not be searching for Microsoft 2013 content in the year 2017, but there will be less people interested in that information than when it was released.

I hope by now you understand the importance of knowing your products, content, and even business components lifespan.

If you can come up with ideas to transform your content into "Evergreen content," content that is timeless, then it will make your blogging business journey easier.

One of the main reasons is that you can create content ahead of time and have it scheduled to be released sometime in the future.

This is exactly what I do!

Typically I will film 10 to 20 blog videos in one weekend and have them scheduled to release sequentially in the future.

This means I have more time flexibility for the next few months as I don't need to create blog content and it allows me to focus on other tasks. I could spend my time creating products, connecting with customers, marketing, or more importantly spending time with my family.

What do you want to do with your additional free time?

CHAPTER 21:
HEADLINES & WRITING CONTENT FOR YOUR BLOG

Once you know your content categories then the next thing to do is create a large list of headlines that you will create content around.

This may be 20 headlines or more. It depends on how far ahead you would like to be with your content. They can be in video form, which is what I personally recommend, they could be audio, written text, images, or a combination. The choice is yours.

Content pieces such as top 10 lists, highly emotional, or controversial topics work exceptionally well. Here are some examples of some enticing and attention-getting headlines:

★ Top 10 mistakes most fishermen make when trying to catch a "monster size fish"
★ Top 50 highly successful entrepreneurs who made over $1 million per year!
★ 5 things you didn't know about sex...
★ How to get the most out of black Friday - DON'T MISS OUT!
★ 5 chicken recipes you'll drool over...
★ Why the iPhone is the WORST phone!

Depending on your niche there is a variety of content types that you can create.

For example, you can create tutorials on how to use Photoshop graphic design software, crazy or interesting celebrity photos that give people a laugh, you can do reviews on products, spiritual insight and advice such as relationship advice if your significant other is cheating on you.

The type of content that you can create is endless!

Remember that while working on the content, you should be thinking about future products that you can present to your target market. Structure your blog content around the products that you have or plan to. This is because those are the people you are trying to attract.

CHAPTER 22:
SPEED OF IMPLEMENTATION

If you want to accelerate your progress and growth one of the best things you can learn to do is to get to the first version quickly.

I am referring to not just your blog website, but your products, marketing strategies, and anything else you want to try.

Get to that first version quickly, but do it strategically without being sloppy.

My point in saying this is not that you want to rush everything you do or get everything done as quickly as possible. However, if you're building a product whether that's writing your own e-book, video informational course, an injection molding product, creating a fashion line, or whatever other product you are creating, you want to get to the first version as fast as possible.

The purpose behind this that is you want to test your idea and see if it works, and if it sells!

You need to know if your customers are truly interested in your product or service quickly before you waste too much time on something that doesn't work.

What I often see with many blog business owners (and many business owners in general) is that they tried to spend months or years building the best product or the best website that they possibly can.

Shortly after they build their super product or website the traffic starts to come and the customers are unsatisfied either with the product, the business, or something else and it flops.

What happens in this case is you wasted months or years of your time to have something that's worthless!

Don't fall into this trap.

I've had this happen to me when I wrote my first few books and even my first few video courses that I created.

The first DVD course I took me almost 5 months to complete and now I can do it in half that time and produce a better quality product.

I should have started with a single DVD or a smaller course. This would have allowed me to ramp up and get some of the kinks out.

My first book took me about six months to write and publish and now in the last year I wrote five books while I was still developing video courses and investing in the stock market!

The thing is when you are learning something new it's going to take you a bit of time to figure out the little nuances. Once you've done something similar you know the process, and it becomes easier.

Take cooking for example. When you know the recipe and it is in the back of your mind, you don't have to think about it or read the instructions. You save time by not having to look things up, measuring, or double-checking.

When you create the recipe through experience you can tell what looks right and what doesn't!

This means at the initial stage, when you are just getting started, focus on getting to the first version quickly because it's about accelerating your speed of implementation.

There will always be things you improve on. Improving and innovation is never ending.

In the big scheme of things, a website or book is never done – they always get revisions, updates, and tweaks. There are always going to be things that you will learn and improve as you progress and get better.

Don't spend months or years perfecting the launch of your first blog website. If you've chosen a bad niche, you want to know this within a month or two that way you can quickly correct your course or change your niche.

Focus on getting to your first version quickly!

Remember that Steve Jobs did not start out with the iPhone 5 the first year they designed the iPhone. They had the iPhone 3G, iPhone 3Gs, iPhone 4, iPhone 4S, iPhone 5, and so on. Business is a process that will continue to evolve just as your blog business will evolve.

You will continue to improve your products and your website. Don't get stuck in the tunnel vision trying to get it perfect the first time.

Listen to your customers and make adjustments along the way as you grow.

CHAPTER 23:
BLOG PERSONALITY & AUTHENTICITY

As you start developing and creating your blog you will develop a personality and style. Keep your blog authentic and don't try to be someone or something it's not.

If you have an authority blog that has multiple authors then you need to know the type of style and personality you want to present on your blog. For this reason it is important to keep expectations clear with your content contributors.

Too often, many bloggers strive to be similar to another popular blogger. This might be a great starting point to find your own personal style such as gathering ideas and examples from one blogger, seeing how different bloggers incorporate stories within their blog, or how someone includes pictures. After seeing all this and gathering your knowledge base you may find a blend and make it your own.

As time moves forward you continue to evolve your style notice the difference from when you started. This is part of the growing process similar to how it takes a newborn horse a few minutes before they can stand on their own legs. At the beginning they wobble figuring out their balance – with time, they run like lightning.

Strong and Extreme voice:

Don't worry if your blog has a strong and extreme voice – there are some very popular blogs that speak out on many different subjects. If on your blog you have a calm and soft voice, you may attract an audience that has a calm temperament.

It may take you some time to find your voice and personality. Using new equipment or mediums to communicate makes it harder because it's new and foreign to you. It's like learning a foreign language. You have to find the groove and the proper tongue position to pronounce the words correctly.

Although if you keep creating content and continue to improve – eventually you will find your voice and your own style.

In the end, don't worry. Continue to improve, get better, and create content.

CHAPTER 24:
THE OVERALL PROCESS TO SETUP YOUR BLOG

In this chapter what I'd like to do is give you a final overview to setting up your blog business. This may simplify some things and give you a blueprint.

When you go through this blueprint keep in mind that there will be sub-steps to nearly all the steps we discuss or mention and that is because you can always take a concept even deeper and further.

For example, there will always be little strategies and techniques that you can tweak and make better such as doing search engine optimization. There are always things that the search engines look for when ranking a website. These are things like keywords, link popularity, and the content that is on your website is a never ending thing to work on and improve.

When looking at this overall blueprint, keep in mind that if you focus on the core, the right foundation, and remember the key principles everything should fall into place.

However if you become attracted to shiny objects, chase various tools and software, or just don't stay focused than it can really hinder your growth.

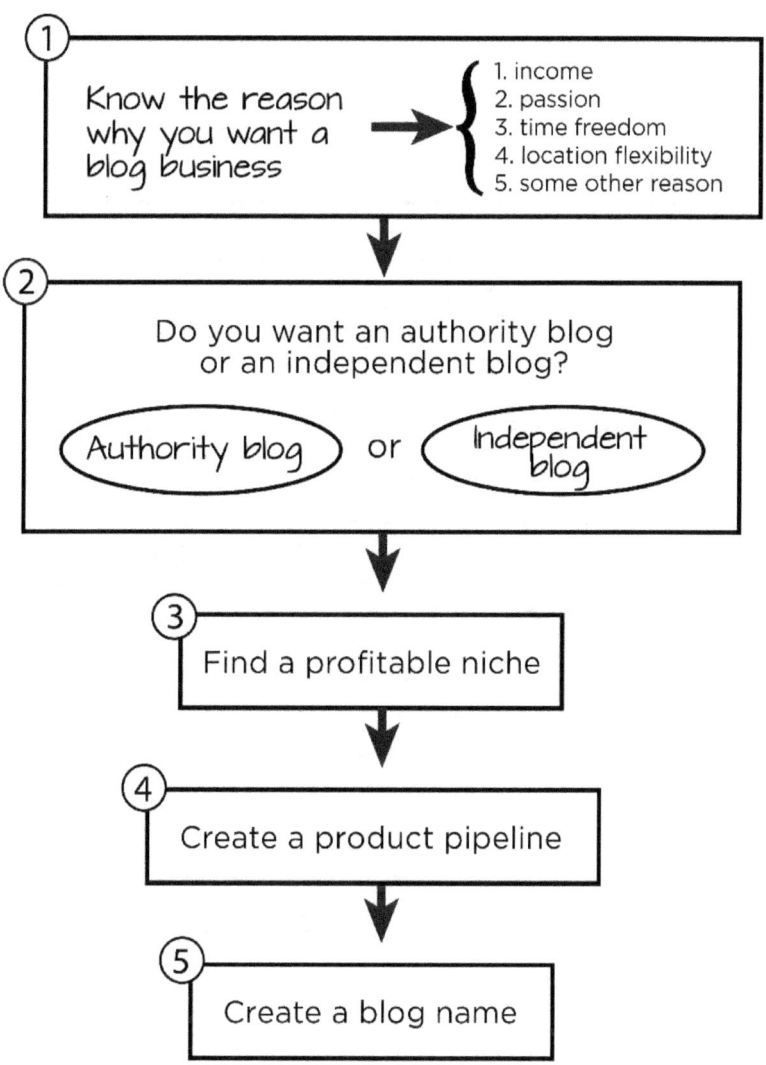

1. Know the reason why you want a blog business →
{
1. income
2. passion
3. time freedom
4. location flexibility
5. some other reason

2. Do you want an authority blog or an independent blog?

Authority blog or Independent blog

3. Find a profitable niche

4. Create a product pipeline

5. Create a blog name

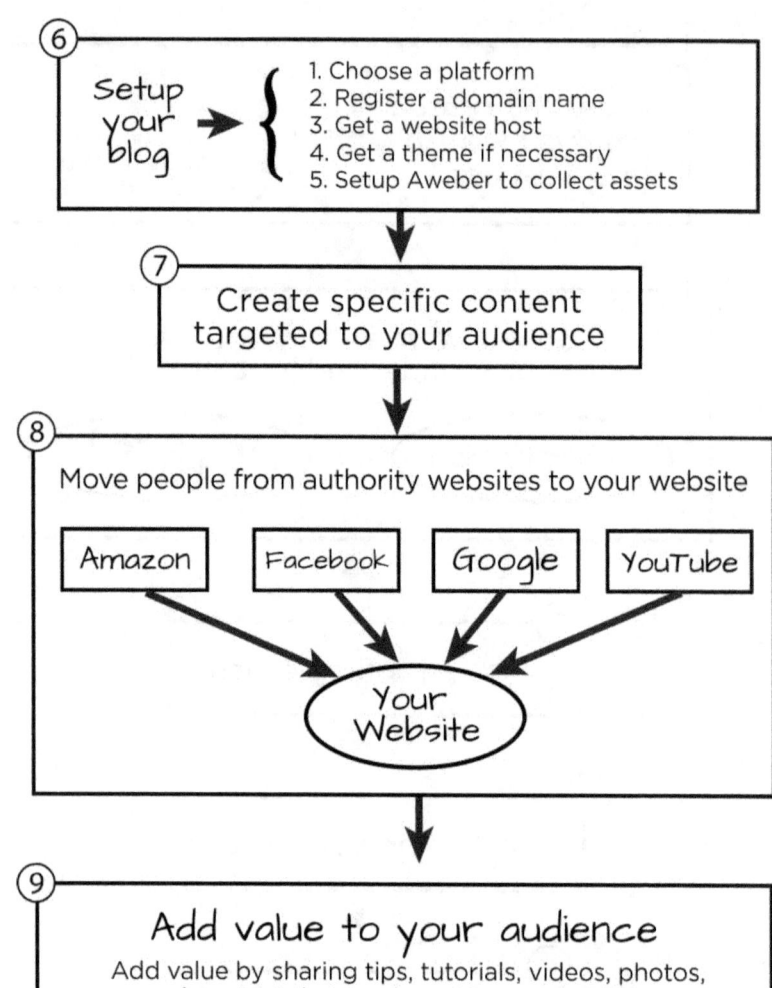

6 Setup your blog →
1. Choose a platform
2. Register a domain name
3. Get a website host
4. Get a theme if necessary
5. Setup Aweber to collect assets

7 Create specific content targeted to your audience

8 Move people from authority websites to your website

| Amazon | Facebook | Google | YouTube |

Your Website

9 Add value to your audience
Add value by sharing tips, tutorials, videos, photos, and content that is relevant to your audience.

(10) # Collect an asset

Building a list of assets such as name, email, home address, or phone number will allow you to develop a relationship with your audience and customers.

(11) ## Build a following

(12) # Present an offer

When you have a following you have a chance to present an offer for a product or service to your audience. You can do this through your mailing list, physical mail, or some other method.

(13) Repeat the cycle and continue to redirect people to your website

Chapter 25:
Questions & Answers

How often should you change the theme of your website?

Too many people get wrapped up with changing the design and theme of their website far too often. The issue is that the blog owners get bored with their design faster than their visitors because as a business owner you tend to look at it more frequently.

Familiarity is a good thing in business. Think of the white and clean lines of Apple and how people are familiar with their designs. Of course design styles change with time, but you want them subtle as your products and blog matures.

For example, if you need to create more categories and there is not enough room at the top of your website, then you may adjust the design to use the left side bar or you could use drop down navigation menus.

Typically for me, I update my website with content and posts as frequently as my schedule is set for. As for my theme or major site adjustments I may update them once a year. This is because new major things have happened such as I launched a podcast or the content simply out grew the navigation or website structure.

When you run out of content ideas what is the best way to come up with more content?

Content in theory is unlimited. You can always go deeper to explain a topic.

You could, of course, go to other blogs to get some inspiration and ideas, but one of the best things to get fresh ideas is to take a breather, get away from the computer, and allow your mind to roam freely.

Idea stumps do happen and it's for this reason why I strive to create content ahead of time. This gives me a few months of buffer time to create more content and allows my brain to relax and gather ideas.

When the moment hits me, then I may do some filming for content creation.

- I find if you break things up into categories such as:
- Top 10 lists
- Looking back at history
- Pros and Cons
- Famous people
- How to
- Tutorials
- Weird things that...
- Etc

This will give you many ideas. Under each category you may have 20, 50, 100 topics. Create an idea bank so when the time comes you can pull from that idea bank and start creating your content.

How long does it take to start generating revenue with your blog?

This is going to depend how experienced you are, the products you are selling, the niche, and your dedication. For this question, I am going to assume you are referring to making your first dollar online.

If you already have your product created or have products you want to sell lined up then it may take a week to setup a blog. Another few weeks to create content for the blog posts, and another few weeks to integrate the products or connect with potential advertisers (probably the fastest way to make your first buck, but not the most profitable).

However, once that is done the battle is not over. You still need traffic to the website and visitors. This can take a bit of time if you don't know proper marketing strategies. Something that I will cover in depth in my next book.

If you don't spend enough time on marketing and let things develop organically it could take 3 to 6 months to start seeing results.

In simple terms, the answer to the question I would say is to give it at least six months, to be on the safe side. For certain other niches it may take anywhere up to one year because not everybody is in a purchasing mood at the exact time.

Think about a purchase cycle - for some people it takes 4 weeks to buy a car, and others buy it in a day because they need to have a car that day to get to work as their last car was destroyed in car accident!

You can of course take the quick route and sell your product on eBay. This would allow you to make your first dollar in a few days however this is not growing your business - it's just getting a quick sale.

When should I quit my day-job to blog full-time?

I would say stick to having a blog business part-time until you can see the payoff is good enough for you to quit your job.

That's the beauty of this business is that you can work part-time and allow it to grow and mature.

If you're making $7 per hour at your job and making $560 per week (working 80 hours a week) then once your blog starts making $400 a week it may be worth it to you to quit your day job because you can work less and have more free-time flexibility.

It comes down to if you would want to work an extra 50 hours per week to make an additional $160 all else being equal.

On the other hand if you are making $20 per hour, work 45 hours a week, that's $900 per week. In this case you may want to wait until the payoff is worth it. This could be $900 from your blog or $700 from your blog.

Whether the finances are critically important or you value the intrinsic things more (like time freedom or location freedom) is something you will have to weigh if there is a large enough payoff for you.

For everyone the situation is going to be different. You have to know how much you value your time freedom, location flexibility, or just doing something you like.

How long should my blog posts be?

Don't think about blog posts in terms of length. Think about the content you produce as interesting or uninteresting.

You can apply this to other areas of life like when you watch TV or movies. Some movies you may sit and watch for two hours or multiple times, and other movies you may want to walk out on.

The reason we sit through long movies is because we find them interesting and appealing to us. If we didn't find them interesting, we would change the channel.

The same concept applies to the Internet. If you can present the information in a way that people become interested in, then they would be happy to read your blog, listen to your podcast, or watch your videos.

If you wanted a simplified answer though, I would stick to a minimum of 500 words per blog post or a few minutes of video content. Give your audience some substance and valuable information from your material - don't make it bland.

Aside from content what other pages should my blog post have?

About Me: a page that is about you. However remember that this page that is about you is really about how you can help your visitors and customers.

Watch this free video lesson to learn how to properly write your about me page:

http://backstageincome.com/courses-business/basics-of-marketing-business/whats-wrong-with-your-about-me-page-how-to-fix-it/

Contact page: the contact page is a way for your customers or visitors to reach out to you if you have questions, concerns or issues with your blog website or product.

Guest author page: If you want to allow guest posts from other blog authors then you may want to have a page that discusses how they can become a guest author or submit blog content to you to share with your audience.

Advertisement: If you plan to have advertisements on your website then you should have a way in which people can see your advertising rates for a way for them to understand your traffic such as the demographics and the psychographics.

Hire Me / Get Started page: If you have services that you offer your visitors then you need a way for them to get started. You don't want to make things difficult for your visitor to be able to purchase your product or service.

404 Error Pages: if someone lands on a page of your website that is not found or they get some kind of error, then you may want to have a custom page for that so they can contact you if there are any unforeseen problems.

Resources or FAQ's: Questions that you get asked frequently such as the tools that you use or what you recommend is another great page to have. This allows people to answer their own questions and saves you time writing emails back and forth.

Does my theme or blog design mater?

The design matters less than the value that you present within your blog.

Remember that it's about adding value to the customer and not about how wonderful your website looks.

If I had two suitcases sitting side-by-side and one was old and ugly, but it was filled with cash. Another suitcase was beautiful, but filled with dirt. Both suitcases were open in front of you - which one would you take?

More likely the suitcase filled with cash, because it would be more valuable to you regardless of its visual appeal.

Even though things may not look great from all angles, you are trying to attract the right audience that wants the value that you have to offer. The design helps in terms of navigation and keeping things clean, but it's far less important than most bloggers think.

What is the most important thing about the layout?

Focus the most on the navigation and making things easy for your visitors to get around your website. This will allow them to stay on your pages longer.

The longer that you can keep them on your website, the more connection you build with them. The more connection that you build the more trust is developed. The more trust you have with your visitors the more likely they are to purchase your products and services.

Should I have a mailing list for my blog?

Absolutely!

Capturing an email address is probably one of the most valuable things that you can collect from your visitors on your blog. Of course you can capture a physical address or their telephone number, which is even better.

How else can you contact your customers in today's digital world? Facebook posts don't show up in everyone's newsfeed, Twitter feeds get buried, but an email is waiting for them once they sign in online.

What mailing list company do you use?

I use Aweber.

Here is my affiliate link http://www.aweber.com/?397816
It gives me a commission if you decide to sign up), but it does not cost you any extra.

I have been using them for years for the reliability and deliverability rates.

You definitely want a mailing list company to send out your newsletters. Doing it from your personal email increases the risk of getting your personal account banned for sending spam. An email list allows people to subscribe and unsubscribe at any time.

It's great for management, for reports, and saves you time with the process.

Is AdSense a great way to make money with your blog?

Most novice bloggers and many incomplete blogging books will tell you AdSense is the way to go or that placing ads on your website is the way to make money with your blog. However AdSense income is pennies compared to the other opportunities available in terms of percentages per visitor.

If your blog gets great traffic then you can make quite a good amount of money from AdSense or something similar, but you definitely make more money by selling someone else's products and getting a commission, or better yet - selling your own product will earn you even more per visitor so long as you get the conversions.

I also believe that since people are staying on your website it is a better win for you rather than the visitor clicking an ad and leaving your website.

On the positive side, I do find that AdSense or advertising revenue is the easiest way to start making money from your blog. Creating and selling your own products is the most difficult.

How much search engine optimization do I need to do?

Today search engines are more advanced and sophisticated. If you have the Yoast SEO plugin and focus on creating a great titles and description tags and build quality links to your website then you should be fine in the big scheme of things.

Personally, I focus on adding and creating value rather than trying to tweak my search engine marketing.

In the end, search engine algorithms will change and you have to continue to chase after the adjustments. It's a game I don't want to play.

On the other hand, if I continue to add value to people then even if I'm ranked extremely low on the search engines those people that really want my material will hunt for an hour trying to find a solution to their problem (the solution that I have).

Should I create social media profiles for my business blog?

Social media profiles these days are useless when you're first getting started unless you plan to promote and advertise through them.

That is because you have no social reputation on them when you are getting started.

You may want to create them to reserve the name, but if you're spending too much time on them at the beginning, then you're probably wasting your time!

These days, Facebook blocks out many of the posts you make to your fans because it clutters the newsfeed. Twitter is a stream of tweets so if someone isn't actively on twitter at the exact moment you post something, your tweet will be at the bottom or buried deep in other tweets.

Once you get bigger and need to connect with your audience through multiple mediums then I would say get yourself a Facebook and Twitter account or other social media profiles. Until then, you might be wasting your time because there are more important things to do.

Note: I don't consider YouTube social media and instead a content platform because you are able to search for content.

Facebook doesn't have results based on search, instead it is more of a time feed similar to Twitter.

How much time will blogging take out of out of my life?

Start blogging slowly in your spare time before you quit your job or give up the things you enjoy.

There is no need for you to make it your full-time job until you are sure it's right for you.

At the beginning it's going to take a bit more time to get things set up and going. I would say find a good time when you're either not in school or have a few days off of work that you can dedicate to get things off the ground.

It may take a week to get that initial setup work complete if you are completely brand new to this industry.

After things are set up and you have your website up and running it may take you 5 to 10 hours of work per week to keep things running smoothly and find your groove.

For example, I may spend 5 hours of filming in a weekend, but it will give me 4 months of blog video posts.

The next weekend I may work on writing a book for 5 hours.

The weekend after that I may work on marketing for 5 hours.

This process continues until I get back to making more blog posts again.

It's important for you to find a cycle or system that works for you. I would say at least give yourself 5 to 10 hours per week if you want to be serious about it to get started.

As your blog evolves may need to spend more time on answering questions or you may want to hire a virtual assistant to help you take care of some of those things.

With time you'll find your groove and it may take you less or more time depending on how you adjust. It also depends on things like if you hire help because you can afford it from the earnings of your blog, or you do it more because you enjoy it so much and possibly even start another blog.

Do I have to learn HTML to be a successful blog business owner?

Not really!

It does help at the beginning stages when you are first creating your blog, but often times you don't need to dig into HTML or CSS.

If you do know HTML and CSS and how to develop your own website is going to save money on hiring someone else to design a template for you (meaning a few hundred dollars saved).

In addition, within one or two years when you need a few adjustments to your website because of it would be helpful to know HTML and CSS, but again you could just spend a few hundred bucks and get things adjusted for you.

I am assuming though if you grew your blog business, you would have cash flow coming in from your blog earnings and it wouldn't be a problem.

Do I need to be a great writer to have a successful blog business?

In the past writing was more important because Internet content was more textual in the written word. Today blogging is not only about writing!

You could be great speaking on video and then have your videos transcribed or have articles created from your videos.

Blogging is about creating content that is beneficial to your target audience. Although it helps to be a good writer, you don't need to be the best of the best to have a great following.

In fact, I've seen some extremely popular blogs that are developed by just regular people talking about everyday topics with poor writing skills. Their popularity stems from their authenticity in their knowledge and information they present to their audience. Writing skills will help, but it's not everything.

How can I make my blog posts more attractive?

Making your blog post more attractive is something that we all want to do. First thing you need to do is sell people to click on your headline and read your blog post.

The way you do that is by having an attention getting headlines. The headline is your advertisement for your blog content. If you get their attention and get them to click your headline, the battle is half won!

After that it's your duty to capture their attention whether through attention-getting graphics, an interesting story, an emotional video, or some other means.

The posts that have the highest and best responses are ones that have the highest emotional value whether that's positive emotions (such as inspirational) or negative emotions such as sadness.

How can I speed up my blogging efforts?

One of the best tips that I can give you to speed up your blogging thinking is to bulk things together and work in block time.

What most people do is they work 15 minutes on their email, and then spend 20 minutes writing a blog post, another 30 minutes on marketing, and they jump around most of the day switching from one task to the next.

The problem is that the switching, or gear shifting, between each task takes time for our brain to adjust, our focus needs to be realigned, and not to mention sometimes the techniques that we have to do are different.

If you're able to focus 5 hours on one task such as writing, or 5 hours on marketing then you will have less wasted time as you switch from one task to the other.

Your focus will be better and the results will come quicker.

Now of course turning off distractions like your cell phone and email are helpful, but I figured you already know these things.

How can I build a bigger email list?

To create a bigger email list you need to create an offer that is enticing for people to give you their email. You can call it a gimmick, a hook, or an offer.

Often time's marketers give away free reports, the 7 secrets to, a free video, or an e-book to acquire an email address.

The email address has become a currency online and it's important that you create a compelling offer to gather this information from your target market.

10,000 emails that are of random people are not as valuable as 200 emails of loyal customers who will buy from you every time you release a new product.

VIDEO COURSE ON STARTING A BLOG BUSINESS

If you are interested in a deeper study on the foundation of building your blog business, you can see my video course:

Build a Blog Business from Scratch!

In this video course I go through many of the concepts in this book in detail as well as show you visually step by step how to choose the right web host, my secrets to finding a domain name, how to get your website up and running, the basics of WordPress, and much more!

This course is over 8 hours long and has 23 video lessons!

Learn more about Build a Blog Business from Scratch at:

http://www.rise2learn.com

BUSINESS BOOKS

★ *Business Launch Pad: Explosive Business Creation and Growth Strategies!*

★ *Marketing Your Blog Business: Increase Your Website Traffic, Build Your Email List & Sell More Products!*

★ To see a full list of business books, visit: http://www.backstageincome.com/books/

BUSINESS VIDEO COURSES

★ Build Your Business Brick by Brick

★ To see a full list of business courses, visit: http://backstageincome.com/products/

FINAL WORDS & THANK YOU!

I wanted to say thank you for reading this book. If you found it helpful or have some comments on how it can be improved, please contact me through my website at http://www.backstageincome.com or send me an email at sasha@rise2learn.com.

Now this book is just the beginning!

If you want to see some great resources that I use to build my businesses then take a look at my website where you can find in detail the exact tools, websites, and the software I use. To see the resources, visit:

http://backstageincome.com/resources/

I wish you great success in your future blogging business journey.

Remember that this is only the beginning and there will be a lot of work ahead. However if you managed to push through and implement some of the concepts and theories that I've outlined in this book then I know you can become successful.

Thank you again,

Sasha

Sasha Evdakov

www.ingramcontent.com/pod-product-compliance
Lightning Source LLC
Chambersburg PA
CBHW051916170526
45168CB00001B/420